The 80-20 Learner:

Shortcuts to Fluency, Knowledge, Skills, and Mastery

By Peter Hollins,

Author and Researcher at
peethollins.com

5

Table of Contents

Chapter 1: Living an 80/20 Life

In 1941, engineer and management consultant Joseph M. Juran became interested in the work of Vilfredo Pareto, an Italian economist and sociologist. Pareto had observed that around eighty percent of all land in Italy was owned by just twenty percent of the Italian population. It was Juran who took this observation and really ran with it, though, claiming that most things in life, not just property ownership, have this kind of unequal distribution. He claimed that **eighty percent of any outcome or phenomenon is actually the result of just twenty percent of the causes.** Juran applied this so-called Pareto principle to many different areas, including economics, mathematics, and industry.

The principle has since been expanded even further to help describe and prescribe a certain mode of distribution in all matters of business, learning, and personal development. Later in his career, Juran himself would use this principle in many loose and ad hoc ways, describing his principle not so much as a law but rather a description of a certain distribution, where **"the vital few and the useful many"** share unequally in a certain phenomenon. He eventually concluded that we could use this principle to our benefit; for example, we naturally become more efficient if we purposefully focus on the "vital" twenty percent instead of the much-less-vital eighty percent.

Today the Pareto principle as it is applied in popular culture is only distantly related to Pareto's original work, but has come nevertheless to represent an important truth about how we can strategically focus our attention for maximum results no matter which area we are working in. Thus it follows that given limited resources, we should prioritize focusing on that twenty percent of our situation that will give us the most "bang for our buck." Of course, the challenge then becomes identifying that twenty percent!

The principle can be applied very concretely to specific issues or to more abstract, overarching concepts. However it's applied, the idea is that by making consistent small efforts in the vital twenty percent, one can achieve substantial success, whether your goal is mastery of an instrument or a language, personal development, or growing a business.

The 80/20 principle is *everywhere*:

- Customer service may spend eighty percent of all their time managing just twenty percent of customer complaints.
- Eighty percent of health care funds are spent on twenty percent of people in a population.
- Eighty percent of a business's sales come from twenty percent of its clients.
- Eighty percent of people tend to use only twenty percent of a phone app's features.
- Twenty percent of software bugs cause eighty percent of all errors.
- People wear twenty percent of their clothes eighty percent of the time.
- Twenty percent of the exercises we do have eighty percent of the impact on our health.
- Analyzing and solving just twenty percent of emerging issues will remove eighty percent of your problems.

- Twenty percent of our relationships satisfy eighty percent of our social needs.
- To be healthy, we need only eat well eighty percent of the time, can "cheat" twenty percent of the time.

The focus of this book is to find out exactly how we can use this principle when it comes to **learning, improving skills, absorbing new information, and boosting memory**. Can this principle help us make the best of our skills and strengths? Can it improve our focus and help us stay lean, minimal, and on track? Basically, can it help us learn better?

The answer is absolutely YES!

However, there is a caveat: **This 80/20 principle has been much misunderstood since the 1940s, and today the concept is often carelessly applied to situations that don't really warrant it**. Many things in life follow this distribution pattern—but not all things. That's why one skill we'll return to again and again in this book is thinking carefully and strategically about *how* to apply the principle—and indeed *whether* to apply it at all.

What 80/20 Learning Really Means

It's important to note that the 80/20 rule is a guideline and **not** a strict mathematical law. The percentages of causes and effects do not necessarily add up to one hundred percent, and the exact figures may vary. The rule merely highlights the imbalanced ratio of effort to results. Furthermore, it doesn't mean that the remaining eighty percent is insignificant or should be ignored. The key is not really to cheat, but rather to find real ways to be more efficient and avoid wasting time on actions that bring only modest satisfaction. The aim is to work smarter rather than harder.

Imagine a student is trying to work their way through an assignment—they've been asked to read five long academic journal articles, but the problem is, they have very little time and need to find a way to do it fast. What's the best thing to do? The 80/20 principle might help them decide that hidden in the pages and pages of data is the most important and essential information—let's say around twenty percent of the total word count. They guess that this info will most likely be contained in the abstracts and concluding paragraphs, and possibly in the figures and diagram. So, they read these bits first. Then, if they have time, they later read the remaining eighty percent. They've successfully applied the 80/20 principle to make their lives easier but also work with limited resources—in this case their time.

But consider another student, who is trying to do the bare minimum to get the highest grade possible in that course. This student knows that their final grade is what matters, and that this is mostly coming from the score on the final exam. They conclude that since eighty percent of their results on this course are coming from twenty percent of the work (i.e., the exam), they should focus exclusively on "learning the exam" and ignore the practical exercises, student discussions, and additional readings. They do this and earn around a seventy percent mark on the exam (which is only a B grade!) but promptly forget the little they've learned because their entire process has been shallow and rushed. They passed the exam, but so what? They learned little. Is this truly the most "productive" way to go about things?

These two examples show us that the 80/20 principle is a helpful starting point, but it's really about helping us think more clearly about:

- What the most important task is
- What our absolute limits are

- What our goals are
- What our priority is—and what we don't really care about

Essentially, **the 80/20 principle is all about cultivating discernment**. When we are discerning, we are able to clearly see through noise and distraction and identify the material, actions, choices, issues, or outcomes that are genuinely the most pivotal. It's about focus and deliberation and avoiding waste and error.

Remember that originally, Pareto simply observed that land ownership was unequally distributed. However, this doesn't mean that knowing this allowed him to predict who would be rich in the future and who would own land. It also told him nothing of why land was distributed that way, or how it might be changed. In other words, his law was purely descriptive.

In the same way, knowing that twenty percent of your products will make you eighty percent of your total product doesn't magically grant you the power to know which products those will be! In other words, knowing that there are powerful and disproportionate causes doesn't mean you are any better at identifying them. It also doesn't mean you instantly understand how to solve the most impactful problems, even if you can identify them.

Sadly, in life there is no "cheat code" that can spare us effort and hard work, but we can apply the 80/20 principle, along with other necessary elements:

- Willingness to constantly observe and update—progress is iterative and evolves over time
- Willingness to pay attention to process, rather than just being carried along by default habits
- The ability to constantly trim away at waste and excess
- The ability to think about our thinking and learn about our learning—i.e., metacognition

The 80/20 rule is powerful—but it needs to be applied intelligently.

Studying and Learning

When applied to being a student, the principle tells us that a significant portion of your success can be attributed to a smaller portion of your total efforts. For example, roughly twenty percent of your studying efforts and time may result in eighty percent of your exam success. The rest of your efforts may have only marginal impact on the outcome ("useful" but not "vital").

Understanding this principle helps you identify the key inputs that have the most impact and allows you to focus and optimize them. By recognizing that a small portion of what you learn in class covers the majority of your exam content, you can prioritize and concentrate on that crucial information. Similarly, you may find that eighty percent of your study time is spent on only twenty percent of the materials you're studying, indicating that you can allocate your time more efficiently by focusing on the most relevant and impactful subjects.

Applying the 80/20 rule in education enables you to avoid wasting resources on less productive activities and instead invest your time and efforts into the areas that yield the greatest results. You can apply the 80/20 concept to the material you're learning, but also to the methods and techniques you're using to learn that material, for example:

Step 1: Create a list of ten study methods

Think about the various techniques you typically use for studying, such as reading material repeatedly, using productivity tools like the Pomodoro technique, taking notes, or highlighting keywords. List these methods, and if you feel you have fewer than ten, explore and adopt additional strategies that suit your needs.

Step 2: Analyze, compare, and rank the methods

Evaluate each method based on factors like ease of use, time consumption, and studying results. Determine which methods provide a better understanding of the material in less time and note them down. Similarly, identify methods that are time-consuming without yielding significant results. After analyzing and comparing, rank the methods based on their effectiveness and efficiency.

Step 3: Identify the top two methods

From the ranked list, select the two methods that consistently deliver the best results for you. These two methods will be the primary focus of your studying. It's important to let go of the other eight methods for now and concentrate solely on these two. By using these two methods consistently, you can accelerate your learning process and achieve better outcomes in a shorter period compared to utilizing other methods.

Reading

Reading a book in its entirety can be a daunting task, especially when faced with a busy schedule or a long reading list. However, by applying the 80/20 principle and adopting a strategic approach, you can extract the most valuable insights while optimizing your reading time.

The principle can be applied like this: Eighty percent of the factual value in a book can be gleaned from twenty percent of its content.

You can guess the limits to this, however. There is no way to adequately "summarize" fiction—in the same way you don't just watch the first and last five minutes of a movie to get the gist! But the 80/20 rule works well with books that are purely data-based—for example, manuals and textbooks.

Prioritize and skim: Start by reading the conclusion or last chapter of the book to understand the author's main arguments or conclusions. Then skim through the entire last chapter to grasp the overall message. This will give you a clear idea of what the author is trying to establish.

Highlight key passages: As you read, use colored pens to highlight key passages that encapsulate the main arguments or provide excellent examples. Look for the overall structure and outline of the book (reading the contents page can help) to get an overview of the material. This not only helps you retain important information but also allows for easy reference in the future. By focusing on these highlighted sections, you can reread the book much faster without going through the entire thing.

Selectively explore: After reading the conclusion and skimming the last chapter, read the introduction to understand the author's intentions and where they are heading. Dip into the rest of the book selectively based on your interests and needs. You can choose to read only the chapters relevant to your objectives, such as finding evidence or gathering examples, or you may decide to explore specific chapters that contain original and highly interesting material.

This approach allows you to save time and focus on the most valuable parts of the book. It's always worth having a clear understanding of *why* you're reading a text before you read it. Prepare yourself with some targeted questions to cue more focused reading.

Learning Languages

The 80-20 approach in language learning allows you to rapidly reach a level where you can effectively communicate and understand crucial concepts without relying on an extensive vocabulary. Any language contains hundreds of thousands of vocabulary words, for example, but a relatively small group of these words get used the most—approximately twenty percent.

Applying the 80/20 approach to language learning could mean, for example, focusing on a curated list of the most commonly used words first, rather than on more unusual or uncommon aspects of the language. Or, if you intend to use the language in a particular setting (for example, work), you may deliberately focus on those phrases that are most likely to help you get things done in your unique job, rather than on random expressions like "I'd like to buy a postage stamp"!

Memory

The 80/20 principle can enhance your learning and retention by forcing you to focus on the most important information. In the context of memory, the principle suggests that a significant portion of the information we encounter is trivial or irrelevant detail. In contrast, a smaller portion holds the key to understanding and retention. By identifying and prioritizing this vital information, we can optimize our memory capacity and cognitive resources.

Identify the most important information by prioritizing the crucial facts, figures, and concepts that you need to learn. It's even better if you can **identify unifying principles** behind these smaller facts. For example, if you're studying history, prioritize the most significant events, influential figures, and key dates that have had a major impact. Use visuals to synthesize information in one place—it's far easier to remember a single data-rich diagram than it is to remember pages and pages of low-density written information.

The key is to be organized. Break down the information into smaller chunks and organize them in a way that makes sense to you. Utilize mnemonic devices, acronyms, and mind maps—for example, when memorizing a list of items, create a mind map by associating each item with a visual image or connecting them through a story (more on this technique later). The visualization and storytelling techniques will help you remember the items in a structured and memorable way.

The Eighty-five Percent Rule

The Pareto principle has plenty of children and grandchildren. One of them we'll explore here: the eighty-five percent rule. As it applies to learning, the eighty-five percent rule basically suggests that **optimal learning occurs when individuals succeed or achieve the correct outcome around eighty-five percent of the time.** This may seem counterintuitive at first—isn't the goal to do as well as you possibly can?

In fact, failure does have a place in learning, and there is some research to suggest that failing about fifteen percent of the time is ideal. This rough estimate is supported by research in both human and machine-learning contexts. According to a recent paper by Wilson, Shenhav, Straccia, and Cohen, various learning algorithms perform best when the training error rate is around 15.87%, which translates to a training accuracy of approximately eighty-five percent.

The rationale behind this rule is that when we succeed all the time, it becomes challenging to identify areas for improvement since there is no contrast between good and bad strategies. Conversely, if we constantly fail, we may struggle to understand what actually works. You may have heard that "practice makes perfect," but in reality, if you are repeatedly practicing the wrong way to do things, you are not actually learning or improving—in fact you might simply be teaching yourself all the wrong things. That's why a better rule is "perfect practice makes perfect."

It is through a mixture of success and failure that we can differentiate between effective and ineffective approaches, allowing for learning and progress. Failure is a teacher, but only in the correct proportions: too much and it can demoralize and confuse; too little and you aren't learning at all.

For a real-world example, we can picture someone trying to perfect their golf swing. They may practice the same movement many times and keep refining it with each attempt. But if they perform every single practice swing perfectly . . . then what? They could conclude that there's no need to keep practicing that swing, but the fact is that they don't know *why* they did as well as they did, or how they could transfer that skill to other tasks.

By the same token, if you kept trying and eight out of every ten swings were an utter disaster, what would happen? Besides you growing increasingly frustrated and upset, you'd also start to wonder what the point of continuing was, since you don't clearly understand why you're failing or what you're supposed to be doing to improve.

But if you're getting around eight or nine of those swings roughly perfect, with just the occasional one wrong, you can gain a much deeper insight into what works and what doesn't. You're in the learning zone. You can *see* that every time you fail, it's because, say, your hips were too stiff in the follow through or you pulled back with your right arm. That's something you can work with.

Your optimal learning lies in being able to focus on that specific area that is actually holding you back—that crucial twenty percent lies in your stiff hips and your right arm. Fail too much or too little, however, and you are unable to identify the important twenty percent and the less important eighty percent. If you succeeded completely or failed completely, you would have no clue that these crucial details about your hip and arm position were actually making the real difference.

Fail zero percent of the time and it leads to **boredom and stagnation.**

Fail more than fifty percent of the time and it leads to **anxiety and overwhelm.**

Finding Your Optimal Challenge Level

We can think of the eighty-five percent rule as the 80/20 rule when applied to failure itself, i.e., **what's the optimal level of failure if we want to learn more quickly and effectively?**

Most of us can understand this concept intuitively when we think of something like a video game—we know that things need to start easier and gradually build, and that tasks need to be a little challenging, but not so challenging that all the fun is drained away. It's the same with learning: We need to find that sweet spot where things are just challenging enough.

Before we do that, however, there are a few caveats: This is a model based on a mathematical theory, so the eighty-five percent is just a heuristic rather than an absolute quantitative truth. Obviously, it will depend on how we define "challenge," and this in turn depends on the task we're doing and what we're attempting to achieve. Some "failures" are different from others; not understanding a word in a language you're learning, for example, is a very different kind of error than fatally crashing while learning to pilot a helicopter.

You may tolerate relatively little challenge at first as you grow in confidence, but end up needing to succeed only seventy-five percent of the time as you progress; some personalities are more resilient to failure than others. Your tolerance for failure or challenge is also not just dependent on the skills you're acquiring—it's about your mood, energy levels, expectancies, biases, and environmental conditions. Your mindset, confidence, and sense of motivation all influence the way you interpret failed attempts—it may be logically possible for you to learn from such a mistake, but only if you approach that mistake with a certain mindset. For some people, a poor mindset means that *even if they reach that sweet spot of the eighty-five percent rule, they are not psychologically prepared to actually learn from it.*

With all that said, exactly how are we supposed to use this information?

Again, this is a metacognitive skill: We need to not just fail or succeed, but step back and become curious about the broader patterns of success and failure. This requires honesty and awareness.

- How often are your attempts (however they're defined) succeeding overall?
- How often are you failing?
- When you fail, are you clearly able to say why?

- When you succeed, are you clearly able to say why?

If you have a lack of clarity over your own process, or else you feel strong negative emotions (frustration, hopelessness, boredom), this may be a sign that you need more insight into how success and failure are featuring in your learning process.

You need to deliberately shape the process so that it includes an optimal level of challenge versus success.

- **Calibrate the level of support you seek:** When practicing problems or tasks, adjust the amount of support you use based on your success rate. If you're getting more than twenty percent of the tasks wrong, consider seeking extra help or resources. On the other hand, if you're consistently getting nearly all the tasks correct, it's time to increase the difficulty and challenge yourself further. This might mean doing things on your own and *not* relying on support.
- **Find tasks at the right difficulty level:** If you succeed every time, chances are the difficulty level is not high enough for you to learn anything new. Seek out the next level of difficulty

and make sure you're finding yourself stumped at least fifteen percent of the time—that's your learning zone. However, fail too often and the difficulty is too high to learn. If this is the case, then you need to grade your tasks by difficulty level, then assign yourself tasks you know you can succeed at approximately eighty-five percent of the time. This balance allows for learning and growth while still providing a reasonable challenge.

- **Find tasks of the right size and kind:** Sometimes it's not that tasks are inherently easier or more difficult, but just that they vary in how they're presented. If you're experiencing too much difficulty, try breaking down tasks until you're working with chunks that feel manageable. In the same way, if things are too easy, "chunk up" and try to do bigger, longer, or more complex versions of the same task. In the same way, you can mix things up by changing format—try a different book, teacher, platform, or modality to increase or decrease the challenge level.

- **Define success appropriately:** Success can be defined in various ways depending on the task at hand.

Consider the specific criteria for success and failure in your learning context. For example, in language practice, success may involve understanding a certain percentage of words or being able to engage in a conversation. Define what success means for you in each task or skill you're working on. If you want to increase challenge, apply more stringent and exacting standards; if you want to lower the challenge, do the opposite and make your definition of success broader and more inclusive.

Training the Ideal Attitude to Failure
Finding your challenge sweet spot is essential if you want to learn most effectively, but there's another reason to change the way you think about failure in general. The reason is obvious: Life is filled with failure!

As you develop the ability to work with and through failure, you are also learning certain emotional skills that help you stay resilient in the face of setbacks and obstacles. There is an old saying that if a child leaves school having experienced nothing but success, then really they haven't succeeded at all, because the one thing they *haven't* learned is how to effectively deal with failure. When they inevitably encounter it in life, they are not prepared—emotionally, that is.

As you work at tweaking your own learning journey so that it challenges you at just the right level, remember to teach yourself what each failure really means. When something doesn't go according to plan, when you're confused or your attempt flops, pause and become aware of exactly what's happening:

- *Have you actually failed?*
- *If so, why?*
- *What can you do better next time?*
- *If you're unsure, who can you ask?*
- *If you lack crucial information, do you know where to find it? How can you get ahold of that information?*
- *Is there anything in your attempt that was correct or usable?*
- *What have you done so far that has worked? Can you do it again?*

Unless you've asked yourself these questions, there's no point in barging ahead mindlessly . . . only to make exactly the same mistake again. If you notice that you have a lot of negative self-talk, irritation, shame, or self-judgment, just tell yourself to set all that aside and become curious.

You fail.

You become aware of a voice that says, "I'm an idiot. I messed that up."

You pause, examine this, and decide to let it go, reminding yourself instead, "No, I just didn't get it right that time. It's normal because I'm learning. Now, what went wrong? Let's get curious about how I can pinpoint exactly what's not working and what I can do better . . ."

Then you succeed.

"Ah ha! So *that's* what the problem was. Good. I'm glad I made that mistake; otherwise I wouldn't have learned that."

In this way, you are learning several different kinds of skills at once: learning the task at hand, but also learning how to learn, and beyond this, learning how to manage your emotional experience around that learning. These secret ingredients come together and create a person who is focused, effective, and resilient.

The Shortcut to Skills Acquisition
You can apply the 80/20 rule to any situation in which you need to acquire new mastery or skills. Picture mastery of that skill as a series of tasks or behaviors—but only around twenty percent of those are really important, while the rest are much less so. It

follows, then, that if you want to arrive at that mastery as quickly as possible, you should focus on that special twenty percent.

Now, while this may seem kind of obvious, the magic comes in because in focusing on the twenty percent, you're actively pulling attention away from all those irrelevant details that could otherwise distract and derail you. In the long run, **what you do might matter just as much as what you consciously choose not to do**. In other words, you become a master at big-picture thinking— when you've got the big stuff nailed down, the details tend to take care of themselves, anyway.

In Tim Ferriss's 2013 TV show *The Tim Ferriss Experiment*, he challenged himself to learn a new skill in just one week. Not just that, but he wanted to learn it to a standard that most people achieve in a year or more. He chose tasks like surfing, parkour, playing the drums, and Jiu Jitsu—and he did it by using the 80/20 rule.

If you're wondering what the hitch is, it's this: Ferriss had an established expert help him find out exactly what the most important twenty percent of any skill really was so he could dedicate himself exclusively to that. In the real world, of course, it's not always that easy to identify this twenty percent. Nevertheless, it does tell us that one good use of limited time and resources is to locate the very best experts we can and bootstrap from the knowledge they've already gained, rather than "reinvent the wheel" ourselves.

Whatever task you're trying to master, first try to find out the essence of the skill being acquired.

For example, you may discover that in marathon running, the single factor that makes the most difference is, essentially, how long you spend running during a single train. Your running shoes, your speed, your technique, the time of day, etc.—none of these is *as* important as the sheer number of hours you can rack up on your feet. That's it. So, focus your attention on that. Whatever you do, don't let doubts or confusion about any of those small details ("Is my foot strike wrong? What should I drink? Do I need to buy new shorts?") hold you back from getting out there and moving.

If you're learning to speak a new language, you may have discovered that the practice that has the greatest impact is frequent, natural speech with native speakers. This alone gives you eighty percent of your competence and mastery. That means that if you want to make the biggest impact in the shortest time, you need to go to the country where they speak that language, and speak nothing but that language for a month, for example. Your approach may be a little scary, and you'll make plenty of mistakes, but your learning curve will be radically different than if you'd stayed at home and poked around on an easy language app on your phone for fifteen minutes a week.

If you're trying to become a better stand-up comedian, and you want to learn fast, then you could look at things this way: What really makes the top performers as good as they are? You might decide that the most memorable comedians are those who are distinctive—i.e., they have their own "thing." You decide that it will take a lot more time and effort to be someone you're not, and much less effort to figure out where you're already unique and skilled, and lean into that. You identify one or two key aspects of a set and work hard on those, simply ignoring those comedic skills that you're not good at. Basically, you're finding and amplifying that twenty percent of your performance that nobody else can do as well as you can—and letting go of the other eighty percent.

For a final example, consider trainee psychotherapists and counselors who are frequently told that one of the greatest predictors of success with clients is not the technique they use, their credentials, or the length of time they've been practicing. Rather, it's the degree of genuine rapport and connection between therapist and client. This means that if you're starting out, your first job is to make sure you are a master at creating good rapport with every new client you meet. Knowing how to do this is just twenty percent of your overall skill set, but it has a disproportionate impact on overall success.

A Warning—Don't Cheat!
That said, a therapist who has zero skills except knowing how to form rapport is going to hit a wall pretty quick! Likewise, simply forcing yourself to run every day or never learning to do a stand-up routine that goes beyond your special gimmick is not enough on its own. But it's a good starting point!

The trick is to find a shortcut and not to scrimp or cheat yourself. Your goal should be to identify those actions and tasks that are sufficient and to focus on those. Your goal is never to bypass effort, to cheat, or to avoid the discomfort of genuine effort or learning. You have limited time and resources, and the 80/20 rule is about budgeting those resources by picking your priorities. But in most areas of life, the eighty percent is less important but not entirely unimportant, and you'll still have to tackle it at some point. Therefore, this approach is a good fit if:

You're really on a deadline—Your job demands that you quickly upskill, you need to lose weight ultra-fast to get a life-saving operation, or there's some other external demand that you have to meet, and it's out of your control.

You have trouble with procrastination—If you throw yourself into a new task and focus immediately on the most important twenty percent, you give yourself the gift of immediate feedback and, hopefully, some positive results. This will feed your confidence and build momentum so that you don't even get the chance to talk yourself out of a new goal or come up with excuses!

You thrive on challenge and competition— In other words, you already know that it's good to leverage your own personality, and you're the kind of person who works better when there's a little pressure.

You're making a BIG change—Occasionally, life demands bold action from us. If you're making a big leap, it might not work to do a slow and steady approach, and you may feel more fired up to grab the thing by both horns and embrace a total transformation. This in itself can be extremely energizing and inspiring.

That said, there are definitely times when it's better *not* to use the 80/20 rule to quickly acquire new skills in this way:

You're hoping to avoid effort—Again, there are no shortcuts in life. The 80/20 rule can make you more efficient, and it can definitely help you avoid doing tasks that have no real value. Just be careful that those tasks really don't have value, however. There's a big difference between trying to learn as quickly as possible, and trying to avoid the learning process entirely—be honest with yourself!

How to Quickly Master Something New

Step 1: Set clear goals for yourself

This needs to be so crystal clear you can almost taste it. You need to know exactly what you're aiming for, what success looks like, and how you intend to measure it when you get there. Make sure your goal is realistic but also embedded in the real world. Have a clear vision of what you want to actually *do* with this skill once acquired; it will make it so much easier to stay the course.

Step 2: Identify sub-skills

Break things down into smaller skills that you can master one by one. If you're learning to make your own clothes, clearly outline all the separate skills you'll need: how to work a sewing machine, how to cut a pattern, how to stitch by hand, etc. (For an extra round of 80/20 rule, take a look at your complete list and see if you can identify only those twenty percent of skills that really matter—start with those first!)

Step 3: Pre-empt challenges

Before you even begin, identify roadblocks and obstacles that are likely to make things difficult, and put something in place to help you overcome them. For example, if you know you have trouble with commitment and motivation, enlist the help of an accountability buddy who will check in with you twice a week no matter what.

Step 4: Build those sub-skills back together

If you're learning the guitar, you might master a few isolated techniques, musical scales, hand positions, etc. until they're seamless; then, as soon as you can, piece those elements back together again. Practice small songs and pieces that combine those skills. Drill and practice the songs until *they* become seamless, then move on to longer songs, and so on.

Tim Ferriss did exactly this with his learning framework, known as DiSSS. It consists of four steps:

- **Deconstruction:** Deconstructing the skill of playing the guitar, for example, would involve breaking things down into smaller components, such as finger placement, strumming techniques, chord transitions, and understanding musical notation.

- **Selection:** In the context of playing the guitar, selecting the crucial twenty percent would involve identifying the most important sub-skills that contribute to eighty percent or more of your desired outcome. This could include mastering basic chords, learning to strum rhythmically, and developing finger dexterity. If you can, it's best to make sure you get this step right by heeding the advice of real experts. What do *they* consider the most essential parts of their learning?
- **Sequencing:** Once you have identified the essential sub-skills, you need to determine the order in which to learn them. In this example, you might start by focusing on mastering basic chords before progressing to more complex chord progressions, scales, and playing melodies.
- **Stakes:** Setting up stakes involves creating real consequences or incentives to ensure commitment and motivation. For guitar learning, you could set up stakes by scheduling regular practice sessions, joining a band or music group that holds you accountable, or even committing to perform in front of others to create a

sense of pressure and motivation to improve.

The DiSSS framework is not all that different from conventional learning methods, but it makes an enormous difference *how* you apply the above steps. Too many people waste enormous energy and motivation essentially learning all the wrong things, at the expense of learning what really matters.

In the guitar example, someone could genuinely want to learn, but wrongly identify what counts as the twenty percent. They may buy an overly expensive guitar because it looks cool, fret about how they're going to pose when they play it, and pick a song that's too difficult. When they sit down and try to replicate it all at once, they get frustrated, making the same mistakes over and over again (and cementing them in). Paired with a poor mindset, wishy-washy goals, and low stakes, the next step from there is obvious: quit.

So, it bears repeating: Not all learning is created equal. Just because you're putting the hours in doesn't mean you are learning. And even if you *are* learning, it doesn't mean you're learning optimally. **Think about your time, your energy, and your motivation as an investment. Where are you going to put it so you get the best return?**

The Framework of Efficiency

Let's consider now how we can apply the 80/20 principle to goal setting itself.

Using the Pareto principle, we can estimate that out of a list of any ten items, around two of them will have disproportionately greater value than the remaining eight combined. However, many people tend to delay taking action on these most valuable and important tasks, focusing instead on less significant ones that contribute little to their success. Prioritizing the trivial many over the vital few is, when you think about it, a form of procrastination.

Naval historian C. Northcote Parkinson wrote an essay in *The Economist* in 1955 where he explained how the British Admiralty and Colonial Office was expanding in size even as the actual numbers of ships on the sea were decreasing. Why? Parkinson went on to make the case that **bureaucracy of all types will always tend to expand to fill its allotted time span**—the so-called Parkinson's law. Basically, he observed what many of us have experienced in daily life in any big organization with a complex hierarchical structure.

But this law doesn't just apply to large, complex organizations—it can play out in the lives of ordinary people. Consider the example of a retired old woman who has very little to do one particular Tuesday, except for post a letter. It's a tiny, trivial task, but somehow she draws it out to its fullest. She takes the longer route walking to the post office, uses a full ten minutes to select just the right stamp, carefully writes out her letter by hand (having a little break in the middle), then makes sure she chats at length with the person behind the counter before leisurely paying in small coins. She walks all the way home again, and when she gets back, it's somehow already 2 p.m. When her neighbor asks her for an urgent favor, the retired woman complains about what a busy morning she's had and how she just doesn't have the time to help!

The story may be an exaggeration, but it carries a grain of truth: If you want them to, small tasks can be made to feel like big ones. These tasks will expand and keep on expanding unless you deliberately draw a ring around them. This "busy work" is sometimes done to fool an employer or because there genuinely is no reason to rush anything, but it's a serious problem if we are fooling ourselves into thinking that we are being effective when really . . . we're just taking half a day to post a letter.

To get around this, it's not so much a question of "working smarter not harder," but rather that the smartness depends on *what* you are working so hard on. The retired woman says she has "no time," but this is not really true—the truth is that she has already used her time on inessential tasks and so doesn't have any left for something more worthwhile.

Another example includes spending hours and hours doing "research" on a project and then feeling rushed because you realize too late that you were also meant to actually produce a written report, not just endlessly *plan* to write one. Or perhaps you spend ages ironing out the details of how you'll achieve something, only to realize halfway through that the entire goal is not quite the right one, and that you should have been taking an entirely different path.

Beware of falling into the trap of becoming ultra-efficient . . . at being inefficient. This is akin to the old woman trying to streamline her day by finding a slightly quicker route to the post office, or waste one minute less on choosing a stamp, when the real timesaver would simply be to forget the letter entirely and write an email! You could spend the afternoon designing a brilliant, color-coded filing system—for a project that never needed a filing system at all. Maybe you force yourself to wake up early to squeeze in a task that didn't need to be done in the first place. Or maybe you throw your heart and soul into achieving a clearly identified goal, only to realize afterward that it doesn't actually help you in any way.

Again, the problem is assuming that *any* old activity is better than no activity. It's seldom about how much of your work, but how targeted, strategic, and focused your work is— and to do that you need a clear goal and the ability to stick to it relentlessly.

A good rule of thumb is to get into the habit of continually asking yourself: **is what I'm doing bringing me closer to my goal?**

Imagine your goal is to walk ten thousand steps every day. Look at the following activities:

- Buying a pedometer
- Investing in workout gear
- Improving your self esteem
- Going for a walk
- Reading a book about the health benefits of walking

Which of these activities brings you materially closer to getting more steps in your day? It's the fourth one—going for a walk. You may have lots of compelling reasons for why the other actions are a good idea and may *indirectly* lead to the overall goal, but if you were forced to choose just one task, it would have to be going for a walk. That is the **only** action that has a direct and concrete link to the goal you've set for yourself.

Sure, the other actions have some value, but be careful about doing those *instead* of the most important task. Always keep it crystal clear in your mind that these tasks are *auxiliary* and should be done only in so far as they make it easier to do what really matters—i.e., buying a pedometer is great, but it will never be the same thing as actually walking. Until you step outside and put one foot after the other, you haven't moved any closer to your goal.

Pick one main goal, prioritize it, and be consistent in working toward that goal every single day. It's hard *not* to succeed if you follow this rule!

Being "Efficient" Means Knowing What's Important

These days, everyone wants to be more productive. But more productive at *what*? You cannot meaningfully talk about efficiency unless you have some metric or standard against which to measure your efforts. You need a clear goal and a clear idea of how every single action you take relates to that goal.

It's a mistake to assume that this is always obvious, or that you'll just naturally know which tasks are more important. The world is filled with distractions and diversions, and it's all too tempting to default to those less important eighty percent tasks than the (often more challenging) twenty percent tasks.

To identify impactful tasks and achieve the best results, try the following steps:

Identify Your Goal

You're probably well aware of the value of SMART goals by now, i.e., goals that are:

- Specific
- Measurable
- Achievable
- Relevant and
- Time-bound

But there's so much more to a truly meaningful goal. Is it something you *really* want—or is it someone else's goal? Is it something you're willing to focus on as a priority until you achieve it? Why do you want this goal and what do you anticipate doing once you've achieved it? Could there be some other, better way to get what you want than this goal? What will likely stand in your way, and have you done what you can to pre-empt and mitigate that?

Categorize Tasks

Make a list of all the tasks you believe you need to complete in a given day or week to achieve this goal. Write down *everything* that you anticipate will take time and effort.

Separate the tasks into two categories: important and unimportant, or must do and should do. This division helps prioritize your focus and attention. The question you want to answer is whether the activity directly contributes to your goal as identified in the previous step.

Let's say you want to learn to code. Your two lists might look like this:

Important:

- Complete a coding exercise for a job application
- Study a new programming language for a project
- Work on a coding project for a personal portfolio

Unimportant:

- Read coding-related articles for leisure
- Watch coding tutorial videos unrelated to current learning goals

On making this list, you might notice that a few of your items need to be broken down and clarified further. For example, what exactly do you intend to do when you assign yourself the task of "study a new programming language for a project"? This may include doing a practical exercise from an online course, reading a journal article from 2001, and spending twenty minutes Googling "how long does it take to learn Python?" This helps you see that the first task is important, the second two not so much. Update your list accordingly.

Quantitative Ranking

Next, look at your list and decide if there are some tasks that simply don't need to be completed at all. Remember, your goal has a better chance of being met if you focus all your time and energy on it and it alone, so be ruthless about things that may be important . . . but are not important right now. Delegate them or cancel them completely.

Then, assign a ranking to each remaining task based on its importance and urgency relative to your goal. Use a scale of one to ten, with ten being the most important. This method allows you to objectively determine the significance of each task and prioritize accordingly.

Example:

- Complete a coding exercise for a job application (Rank: 10)
- Study a new programming language for a project (Rank: 9)
- Work on a coding project for a personal portfolio (Rank: 8)
- Do a practical exercise from an online course (Rank: 7)
- Read coding-related articles for leisure (Rank: 3)
- Watch coding tutorial videos unrelated to current learning goals (Rank: 2)

Ordinal Ranking

Focus on the "twenty percent" of items, which represent the highest-value tasks that have the most significant impact on your long-term goals. This may feel tricky to do because eight tasks may feel like more than two, for example, but remind yourself that the higher-ranking tasks will bring you much greater results *for the same amount of time spent.* That means that even if you did twice as many of the low-ranking tasks, you still would not achieve the same outcome.

Start by completing the highest-ranking tasks first, then move on to tasks with medium impact, and finally tackle the ones with low impact. This approach helps maintain focus, prevents distractions, and avoids burnout by ensuring you allocate your energy effectively. You may find, however, that you often don't get to the medium- and low-impact tasks before a new, high-impact one emerges and demands your attention. That's why it's important to regularly appraise your to-do list in this way—yesterday's priority might not be today's, and vice versa.

If you only have one hour to spare, then pick the very highest-ranking task you can and do your very best with it. If you're exhausted or you've completed all the most important tasks for the day, then take it easy with the lower-ranking tasks. You already know that you don't have to pour your heart and soul into these tasks in quite the same way. By applying both quantitative and ordinal ranking methods, you can identify the most impactful tasks and ensure that your efforts are directed toward high-priority activities that align with your goals.

Summary:

- In short, the Pareto principle or 80/20 rule states that eighty percent of all outcomes arise from just twenty percent of causes, i.e., in many phenomena there are "the vital few and the useful many." We can use this principle by focusing on the vital few and de-prioritizing the useful many.

- We can apply this principle to learning, improving skills, absorbing new information, and boosting memory. We need to avoid carelessly applying the rule to situations that don't warrant it, and learn to think strategically about how and why it works for each situation.

- You can apply the technique to selecting the most effective study methods and techniques (make a list of ten and choose only the two most effective ones), reading, learning languages, and memorizing new material. By identifying the most useful, relevant, or unifying principles behind anything you learn, you stay streamlined and organized.

- A related law/principle is the "eighty-five percent rule," which states that optimal learning occurs when individuals succeed or achieve the correct outcome around eighty-five percent of the time. Through an optimal mix of success and failure, we can differentiate between effective and ineffective approaches, allowing for learning and progress. Deliberately shape your learning process so that you have the optimal level of failure by varying the size, type, and difficulty of tasks, and the support you receive to complete them.

- You can apply the 80/20 rule to acquiring new skills. What you do is as important as what you choose not to do. Your goal is not to bypass effort, cheat, or avoid discomfort but to wisely budget limited resources.
- Master new skills by setting clear goals, identifying and mastering smaller sub-skills, pre-empting and preparing for unavoidable challenges along the way, and piecing the subskills together again as you go.
- To be efficient, constantly ask yourself: is what I'm doing bringing me closer to my goal? Pick one SMART goal, prioritize it, and be consistent in working toward that goal every single day. Hack away at the inessential.

Chapter 2: Keep Things Lean

Sometimes people think of their brains like blank slates so that whenever they want to learn something new, they are starting "from scratch." They may feel like they know nothing and are starting as absolute beginners, so they consult all the right masters and experts and diligently follow the path they outline. There's nothing wrong with this approach. However, it fails to take advantage of something that is frequently underestimated: the value of your own prior learning.

In this chapter, we'll be looking at an underappreciated way of looking at the learning process, which focuses on what you *already know* . . . and how to leverage it. In a way, it's a clever application of the 80/20 rule:

With any new concept or skill, **try to identify the twenty percent that is genuinely new and unfamiliar to you, and deliberately leverage the eighty percent that you probably already know something about**. Being a "minimalist learner" is therefore about building on whatever existing foundations you have—and there's more there than you think!

What You Already Know Is the Key

Think about all the things you've already learned in life, starting from the day you were born. It's a *lot*. Your brain is bursting with this gathered and synthesized knowledge. In fact, cross-referencing every new piece of data it encounters against this vast library of pre-existing information is exactly how it learns in the first place.

For example, as a child you learn that the furry brown creature that barks is called a dog. Later you encounter another furry creature that barks, but this one is white. When you're informed that this one is *also* a dog, you update your internal mental schemas to reflect the fact that different members of the class "dog" can come in different colors. Perhaps you start to imagine how many other colors dogs can be, and whether this general rule can be extrapolated to other animal classes, too.

You do not need to understand formal logic to make this leap. You don't need to start from scratch, either, running through a complicated diagnostic to figure out what animal you're looking at. Learning that some dogs are white is not something you are ever taught, but something you infer purely from what you already know. Whenever you encounter something a little different (e.g., the new idea of being white in color), this constitutes the crucial twenty percent that needs to be integrated somehow into the already-existing eighty percent framework of the category dog. It makes sense, then, that your learning process should capitalize on this ancient and pre-existing learning software that you already come installed with!

Here's where the 80/20 rule comes in: Your brain typically processes things it already understands very quickly and with minimal effort. For example, every time you encounter a new dog, your brain is not processing every single bit of information you take in—it's only "learning" a few extra bits that make *this* dog different from your general working model of a dog.

When something different happens in your world, and your brain encounters something novel and memorable, you immediately focus your attention more fully on it. When you've "learned" that new thing, it becomes somewhat automatic and less demanding of your cognitive resources. This is why learning to drive was difficult and all-consuming, whereas once you knew how to do it, you could drive to work on autopilot, even arriving at your destination with no real memory of how you got there. Then again, if the roads were unexpectedly closed and you had to find a completely new route to work, you'd start to pay attention again because you'd be in learning mode again.

Think of these two different capacities as long- and short-term or working memory. Your working memory is like a desktop where you are actively focusing on a task. Your long-term memory is like a filing system under the desk where certain memories and associations are stored, ready to be retrieved by certain cues and triggers.

Teachers know that a student has the best chance of grasping a new concept if they can connect it meaningfully to concepts they have already mastered. **New information has to be fully integrated into pre-existing information—like building new layers on**

an older foundation. Without connecting to the older foundation, new knowledge lacks context and meaning and is soon forgotten. For example, you have many instances of "learning" about a range of different animals of all colors who all bark, but you cannot remember and contextualize them so they become part of the same concept: "dog."

One reason that connecting new learning to old learning works so well has to do with *cognitive load*. Your brain can only process so much; beyond that limit it struggles. Cognitive load theory tells us that new information is processed in the brain's working memory, which has a very limited capacity indeed. You can imagine this like your work desk being rather small, or else imagine that the brain is like a narrow-necked bottle: Working memory is like the bottle neck—only small pieces can enter in at one time, but once it's in there, far more can be stored for later.

So how can we use all this to lower our cognitive load and learn more quickly and effectively?

Start with What You Know
Begin any new learning endeavor by recapping what you already understand—

or perhaps what you've already absorbed from a previous session. This simple act of asking your brain to dig around for any relevant pre-existing information actually primes you to learn more effectively and approach your process with more agency and focus.

One way to do this is to scribble out a mind map of everything you can think of—don't be tempted to Google information. If you're unsure, put question marks next to information and draw tentative links between concepts. You may find you want to write down a few targeted questions—what are the things you most want to find out next? What missing piece of information will help you fill in the gaps or activate this mind map? This is the 80/20 rule in play once again: Ask yourself what the single greatest unknown is for you (that crucial twenty percent) and how you might go about learning more.

The great thing about making this kind of mind map is that it serves not only as a way to organize and shape your learning, but as concrete visual proof of just how far you've come. As you read and learn, your brain will unconsciously be looking for ways to fill in the gaps and find answers to your questions. You can add these to your map, and as you go along you'll develop new questions to add. Beginning with what you know (or don't know!) as a foundation, you'll gradually build a scaffold of new information, onto which you can build more connections and associations. But because you're piercing your knowledge together in such a responsive and organic way as you go along, you're engaging with the material on a much deeper level than if you'd just made a summary at the end or used someone else's mind map.

Create Meaningful Connections

Someone might be telling you a long story about Peter Tuchman, someone you've never heard of before. Then they say, "He's like the Einstein of Wall Street." With that simple, seven-word metaphor, you suddenly know a lot more about him, don't you? That's because you've connected something you had no clue about (Tuchman) to something you did (Einstein).

There are lots of ways to directly connect new information to old, however. Importantly, **you don't have to make these connections logically or cognitively—*emotional* connections are also extremely powerful.** When learning about a complex biological or chemical process, for example, you could make up a little story where each molecule or protein is a character that resembles someone from your real life. It's far easier to remember the story if your take is filled with love, betrayal, intrigue, and scandal than if it was merely dry facts about boiling points and so on.

Similarly, when making mnemonics to help you recall new information, remember that you are far more likely to remember something that personally relates to you and your world, or something that is shocking, humorous, vivid, or bizarre. The more you can make new information come alive for you, the more quickly it will become part of your world. Make novel things feel familiar and relevant and you will never forget them.

One interesting tip is to study different aspects of your material in different rooms, or even experiment with different chairs, pen colors, or background music to make deliberate and distinctive associations. You might more easily recall something you've read if you can connect it to a very specific Tuesday afternoon when it was raining and you were at a friend's house and there was a certain TV show playing quietly in the background and you could smell coffee in the next room. Think of all these sensory memories and associations as tags or handles that allow you to retrieve a memory from storage—the more of them you have, the better. That way, even if one association fails, you have many others to draw on.

Get an Overview of the Study Material

Let's say you have a history exam approaching, and one of the topics you need to study is the American Civil War. Before diving into specific details, it's beneficial to get an overview of the study material. Start by skimming through the relevant chapters in your history textbook, paying attention to headings, subheadings, and key points. Look at the table of contents to understand the organization of the content and the major themes covered.

As you browse, try to answer general questions about the Civil War, even if you are unsure of the exact details. For instance, you might ask yourself about the causes of the war, significant battles, or key figures involved. As you read, you're then primed to search for these answers. Scribble questions, little diagrams, or comments in the margins as though you were having a conversation with the material, or see if you can pause before each section to guess what's coming next.

This overview helps you develop a mental framework and roadmap for your study. It keeps you actively engaged with material, pre-empting new information and consciously integrating it with a working model as you go. This is "active reading" at its best. Continually repeat this process throughout your learning journey to maintain a clear understanding of the overall structure and direction of the subject matter. It's like ensuring that you're gradually working with what's on your work desk, and steadily filing it away in the cabinets beneath, one concept at a time.

To finish any study session, stop and appraise what you've done. Compare it to your goals and what you intended to achieve in that session. If you've scribbled down a mind map in the beginning, return to it and check to see if there are any questions you can now answer.

You are far more likely to remember information that you've taught yourself in this way than information you just passively took in! What's more, you'll get a clear sense of progress and give yourself the opportunity to evaluate your study method. If you've achieved what you set out to, congratulate yourself and take a break. If after an hour you can't honestly say you've made any headway, that's a clear sign that something needs to change!

Become Your Own Minimalist Teacher

Cast your mind back to when you were in school and try to remember how you spent each day. Think about the moving around from classroom to classroom, the PE lessons, the preparations for exams, the pop quizzes, the teacher droning on and on, lunch in the cafeteria, all the teenage dramas and politics, schedules, trigonometry homework . . .

Now look at all this and ask yourself which parts genuinely held real-world value, helped you learn and develop, and gave you applicable skills you use to this day. If you're like most people who've gone through conventional schooling, you'll probably say this amounted to way, way less than twenty percent. At times, it might have felt that we were all in school basically for its own sake, with many of its associated rules and rituals having only the faintest connection to genuine educational outcomes.

And yet, when many of us try to learn as adults, we still tend to mimic all the same practices we learned in school. Maybe we sit down with a highlighter and read a textbook, or force ourselves to study in hour-long chunks. But why? In this chapter, we'll be considering just how much of what we've been taught about learning is actually necessary . . . and how much can be discarded as belonging to that eighty percent.

Minimalism is an increasingly familiar concept, but we can apply its principles to education and our professional lives, too. The idea is not to be spartan and self-punishing, or to achieve some aesthetic sense of Zen-like calm. **Rather, it's about thoughtful, values-driven, conscious consideration of the *value* of things—and an attempt to structure life to match.**

Even if we have a clear idea of our goals and priorities, that eighty percent can still get in the way in the form of clutter and distraction. Minimalism is a way of constantly clearing away at this inessential element so that the essential is constantly shining through. In other words, it's about decluttering everything:

- Our desks and study spaces
- Our digital lives
- Our minds

- Our schedules and to-do lists
- Our media consumption
- Our diets
- Our work practices
- Our spending habits
- Our beliefs and attitudes
- Our living situation and lifestyle

. . . and the list goes on. Decluttering on its own, however, is not a moral act and has no value—rather, we declutter because we are trying to achieve the state of calm, reflective balance that comes with removing the noise from life. Exactly what is decluttered will vary between people because people have different goals and values. **Minimalism is about the clarity and purpose behind what is removed and what remains, and not strictly about *what* you're choosing to keep.**

Decluttering Step by Step

Your Outer Space

Your material environment is a reflection of your mental and emotional one. Take a look at the space where you intend to learn and try to see it with neutral eyes. What kind of a person works and studies here? What thoughts and feelings does it inspire? What kind of actions and behaviors does it support, and what kind does it discourage?

You might like to consider individual items in your learning space. Pick up one or two and hold them in your hands. In the same way that you have a goal you are focused on, ask yourself what this thing's goal is. What purpose is it meant to serve and how successful is it at performing that job? Do these goals and purposes align with your own? Think about how necessary this item is, whether it's in the right place, and the kind of impact it has on you.

Now, the idea is not to get carried away with a depth analysis of every pen and pencil in your office, but with fresh eyes you can start to understand whether your environment is broadly *for* your learning or *against* it. You might make the decision to clear away some items, buy new and more appropriate ones, make some space, clean things (this is huge— what is the psychological message behind dirty learning materials?), or change the seating, lighting, and temperature control.

Your Inner Space

In the same way as you carefully considered a few items in your study environment, turn inward and consider the mental and emotional "items" in your inner space. Here are a few questions to help you identify these items. The idea, again, is to compare these things against your stated goal—are your attitudes, beliefs, feelings, assumptions, etc. *for* or *against* your stated goals? How essential are they, really? Are they part of the twenty percent or the eighty percent?

- *Attitude and mindset*: How are you approaching the learning process? Perhaps you see it as an insurmountable challenge, a new possibility, a threat, a boring chore, or something you're doing because you're supposed to? Complete the sentence "learning is . . ." and brainstorm a few spontaneous answers. You may discover that you consider learning something you're forced to do, or something like an obligation or a sacrifice. Maybe you see personal development as a "way out." Without judgment, explore these attitudes.

- *Thoughts*: About the new thing you're learning, about yourself, about the world. Take a moment to do an inventory of the positive and negative thoughts you're carrying into the learning process, such as "I'm a fraud" or "I can do this."

- *Feelings*: Are you excited, curious, encouraged? Are you bored, resentful, and tired? Take stock.

- *Fears*: What are you worried about? Many of us are afraid that we don't have what it takes to be better. Some of us are afraid that maybe we *do* . . . and then what?

- *Habits*: The momentum of how we've always done things can keep us from doing things in a different way. What habits, routines, and lifestyle choices are you working with?

- *Beliefs*: This one goes a bit deeper. Some people unconsciously limit themselves because they believe that they're not worthy to strive for an ambitious goal, or they hold back because they fear that shining too brightly will make others feel bad. Maybe you are afraid to try because you believe that you're less deserving, less resilient, less intelligent than others. Or maybe you're telling yourself a story about the kind of person you are, and though you have dreams, you secretly feel that they're not for someone like you.

The point of these questions is not to get bogged down in pointless psychoanalysis. Rather, you're looking at each and every thing that's in your mind, and asking, "Does this serve me? Is this brining me closer to my goal?" If not, you can happily set it aside (of course, doing so may take a little practice—mental clutter is more stubborn than physical clutter!).

Is a certain attitude or behavior holding you back?

Your Work Space

Bearing in mind what we've already learned about long- and short-term memory, the final step is to take an objective look at your informational processes and how they're organized. Your learning journey will entail moving through a curriculum you've designed yourself—i.e., walking a path through the big wide world that is packed with *lots and lots of information*. You don't have enough time or brainpower to take it *all* in, so you need to be discerning. Your process is a focused minimal one when you are taking in what is valuable, appropriate, and useful toward your goals, and ignoring or discarding what distracts, derails, or undermines.

Ask yourself:

- *Is this task I'm doing directly bringing me closer to the goal or not?*
- *Is this a "filler" task or "busy work"?*
- *How would my process look if I just dropped this task? Do I lose much?*
- *Can I achieve what I want more quickly or more effectively in some other way?*
- *Can I make this task more tailored to fit my goals?*

In today's information-soaked world, we are all never very far from a screen that carries us into a world of endless distraction and noise. Get into the habit of noticing every time your attention is pulled this way and that way. Then ask, is this book/website/podcast/talking head/news story/movie/video game/phone call/email/YouTube video keeping me on my path toward my goal?

Always remember that **your attention and awareness are your most valuable resources—and that you get to choose how you "spend" those resources**. Are you spending it on tasks you know will help you, or are you throwing it away on things that bring nothing to your life?

One of the biggest ironies is that in the attempt to be more streamlined and productive, we can actually end up buying into all sorts of gimmicks. But do you *really* need a new bullet journal method, a forty-five-minute video about someone's opinion on something, a complicated infographic, a new mediation technique, and so on and so on? Are you really being minimalist if you get stressed out and need to spend a week "decluttering" in just the right way? Instead, just ask yourself:

What is the least that needs to happen for me to make concrete progress toward my goal?

Then immediately take ACTION in that direction. Forget everything else for the moment and just do that task. You always have the control to thoughtfully select relevant and meaningful resources and minimize the usage of materials and techniques that hinder your progress—no matter how popular they are!

A minimalist approach to learning encourages simplicity and flexibility in the process of acquiring knowledge. It advocates for a balanced and manageable intake of information, ensuring that the mind is not overwhelmed or exhausted by an excessive amount of data. In other words, you're doing the *opposite* of so much of what you learned in high school!

Minimalism in self-directed learning involves a mindful approach to knowledge application. Instead of passively consuming information, **actively engage with the content and reflect on its relevance to real-life situations or practical contexts.** Trust yourself, your own values, and your judgment on what is important and what isn't.

Apply what you've learned through projects, exercises, or discussions to make your learning more meaningful. By focusing on the practical application of your knowledge, you can optimize your learning outcomes and retain information more effectively. You are a student, but remember, you are also your own teacher, and there is an authority in that. Take charge of your learning and develop discipline and regular reflection.

Don't fall back into automatic habit and empty routine, or allow other people's ideas about what learning should look like to hijack your process. Continually assess and reassess your learning environment, plan, and progress to ensure that you are staying focused and avoiding unnecessary distractions. And when you have identified something that feels irrelevant, discard it without guilt or a second thought. By doing so, you are crafting a rich, meaningful learning experience that actually gets you to where you want to be.

Minimizing Information Overload

The moment you decide you want to learn a new skill or acquire knowledge, something interesting happens: A whole new world of information seems to open up, and before you know it you're flooded with books, journal articles, videos, audio recordings, how-to guides, and on and on.

Today, we are blessed more than ever before to have easy and immediate access to vast quantities of educational material—much of it for free. But there's a flipside to this abundance, and it's the fact that very quickly, you can become overwhelmed, even losing track of what you were trying to do in the first place.

In this sea of information, we need to *constantly* remind ourselves that a portion of all data we encounter will be irrelevant to our goals, outdated, inaccurate, inappropriate, or flat out wrong. Our job, then, is to move through this eighty percent and continually identify the twenty percent that matters most to us—without getting too bogged down in that sorting process itself (because yes—endless optimizing and organizing can quickly become an eighty percent activity!).

What you need is a regular, low-effort way to manage the volume of information coming your way:

Step 1: Identify exactly WHAT you need to know

Again, we are in the realm of goals. *What do you need to know? Well, whatever is necessary to help you take the next step on your learning journey.* You need to know only that . . . everything else can wait. If you know with absolute clarity how you are spending the time from noon until 1 p.m., for example, then when something comes along to steal your attention, you can easily ask yourself, "Given my goal for this hour, do I need to know about this or not?"

Too many of the sources of information that come our way these days are designed to be attention-grabbing, sometimes purely on emotional grounds alone. When you pause and look closely, there is not all that much genuine content there in the first place. The very alarming news headline contains, on further investigation, a collection of arbitrary opinions that don't add in any way to your life. The TV show that at first seemed entertaining is almost identical to ones you've watched before, and the "additional reading" your tutor prescribed is only vaguely connected to your learning outcomes . . . but will take fourteen hours to read.

Before you launch into a new piece of information, pause and measure it against your goals. If it does relate, continue to read or watch with a very clear idea in your mind about what you're hoping to get from it. At the end of an article, for example, what valuable, actionable piece of information will you possess that you don't possess now? As you read, actively *look* for that piece of information.

Step 2: Identify HOW MUCH you need to know

Have your own "informational boundaries." Having a definable reason for why you're reading something is good, but you also need to put a cap on just how much of that data you take in. Remember that you are taking in information for a reason. Is your reason just to increase general knowledge? Is it to help you solve a problem? Is it to better inform the decisions you're making?

Knowing the reason means you can take in *only* the amount of information that will help you achieve that goal—and then stop. Sometimes you can get away with a quick skim or reading a summary; other times you'll need to read with more depth and understanding. But in either case, regularly pause to ask if you've actually gleaned enough information to answer the question you went in with. This is why it's so important to know what you're doing *before* you get swamped with information. Knowing when to stop researching and data-gathering is crucial to cutting down on feelings of overwhelm.

Step 3: Actively discern the VALUE of what you're looking at

Become a conscious consumer of information. Don't just take something in passively—break it down, analyze it, ask questions, and become curious about how it's organized and why. How valuable is this information, in absolute terms but also as it relates to your own values and goals? Who created it and why? How complete, accurate, and relevant is it? Does the author have the credentials, experience, or authority to make the claims they do?

With laser-like focus on your goal, you can quickly appraise if something is worth your time and attention, and if not, quickly move on, never allowing yourself to get overloaded with poor-quality information. If you have more than one high-quality source of information, choose the *best* one and ignore the other one. If, for example, you're getting bogged down with endless trade publications and articles, subscribe instead to just a single update newsletter that contains highlights from all of them.

As you're doing this, you can also begin to immediately pick out the most important parts. Even before you dive in, read headlines or content lists, skim diagrams and tables, look at abstracts or summaries, and get a sense of the overall structure and argument of any piece of information. Similarly, try to quickly find areas where this piece disagrees with your own view or with another author or idea. Zoom in on that and you can often skim past other background and contextual information—the 80/20 rule tells us that only twenty percent of what you're looking at matters. How will you quickly find out what the twenty percent is?

Are You Overwhelmed . . . or Scared?

Before we move on, it's worth pausing and considering that not all feelings of overwhelm come literally from too much information. **Overwhelm can be an *emotional* experience as much as a cognitive and practical one. It arises not because we're facing too much data, but rather that we don't quite feel up to the challenge of processing that data.**

The learning experience consists of many different threads running in parallel—as you are learning new information and skills, you are simultaneously engaging on an emotional level with the process itself, and developing the meta-skills of time management, good mindset, discipline, and so on. Particularly if you are learning something new late in life, or challenging yourself well out of your comfort zone, you might find a bunch of fears appearing—fears that you are not good enough, not talented enough, not tough enough, or not able to adapt quickly enough.

Some people can approach adult learning with the hang-ups they first developed in school, where the stress of performing in exams dented their confidence, or cemented a lifelong belief in how intelligent they were and just what they were capable of. Perhaps you're one of those people who thinks you're smart but performs poorly in an academic setting. This automatic sense of resistance to learning something new as an adult can set up nasty self-fulfilling prophesies, though, because we never get the chance to prove to ourselves that we *can* learn and grow, no matter how it went in the past for us.

If you suspect your feelings of overwhelm have something to do with a bigger fear of learning in general, don't worry—you're not alone. Reframing your thought processes around learning simply requires a little curiosity and experimentation.

- Think of upskilling not as a boring, scary thing, but as a luxury and a treat that you give to yourself because you care about being the best you can be.
- Forget about being externally ranked, appraised, and graded, and focus instead on the *process* of learning something new, not the *outcome*.
- Start to tell yourself and others that you relish learning and that you consider it

a lifelong activity—not just something you do to get to the end.

Adopt a problem-solving mindset: If things seem too big and intimidating, break them down until they don't feel so big anymore. If you feel rushed, slow down a little, take a breath, and just focus on the next step, not the next twenty. If you're uncomfortable with technology or feel like a lack of skill is holding you back, ask what the very first step is to take to confidently seek out that knowledge for yourself.

To overcome the fear of studying and learning, it is important to follow a few tips:

Identify the cause of your fear: Determine what is causing your fear of learning. Is it the fear of failure, judgment from others, or past negative experiences? Understanding the root cause will help you address it effectively. For example, you might realize that your fear of learning how to paint stems from the belief that you have no artistic talent or that you will not be able to create anything worthwhile. By identifying this fear, you can address the underlying self-doubt and negative beliefs that are holding you back.

Take control of your fear: Recognize that your fear will not go away on its own. Seek expert advice if needed and take action to confront your fear. Embracing a new career or course may require letting go of the familiar and redefining your professional identity. It can be intimidating but necessary for growth.

In the case of fear of learning how to paint, taking control means actively seeking out resources and support to overcome your fear. You can start by joining a painting class or workshop where you can learn from an experienced instructor and interact with other aspiring artists. By surrounding yourself with like-minded individuals and receiving guidance from professionals, you can gain confidence and reassurance that you are on the right path.

Break it down into incremental steps: If the idea of pursuing a full qualification seems overwhelming, start with a short course on a subject of interest. Consider your transferable skills and prioritize the critical skills needed for success. By taking smaller steps, you can build confidence and gradually tackle more challenging courses. Instead of overwhelming yourself with the idea of becoming a proficient painter overnight, break down the learning process into smaller, manageable steps.

Start by experimenting with basic brushstrokes, color mixing, or simple still life subjects. Set small goals for yourself, such as completing a small painting within a certain time frame or mastering a specific technique. As you achieve these incremental goals, you'll build confidence and motivation to tackle more complex aspects of painting.

A Trick for Time Management AND Anxiety Management

If you find yourself feeling overwhelmed (especially when it's 3 a.m. in the morning and you can't turn your brain off!), here is a technique that can help you cut away at the inessential and get back in touch with what is important.

Have a little "worry notebook" where you deliberately attempt to catch and contain all intrusive thoughts, worries, questions, or demands that spontaneously emerge and pull on your attention. You can have a literal notebook as well as a separate folder on your desktop for digital items. When you're focusing on just a single task or idea, and you notice that something pops up to stress you out or distract you, immediately set this idea aside by writing it in your notebook, or by putting a link or attachment in your folder. Tell yourself as you do this that you will return to this idea later, when you've finished focusing on what's important.

Anxiety from information overload often comes from the feeling that we might be missing something important and time sensitive. But if you note something down, you're telling your brain that you won't forget and that you will deal with this idea fully—but *not yet*. You can worry as much as you like, but do it on your own schedule! Tell yourself, "Thanks for bringing my attention to this, brain. I've made a note so there's no need to keep reminding me. I'll take a look at it, but later. Right now, I'm doing XYZ."

This is a technique called **worry postponement**, and it helps you maintain clearer boundaries around intrusive, distracting, or irrelevant information. You assign yourself a deliberate period of time where you'll look at your worry notebook or folder and take concrete action on those items. For example, you can schedule fifteen minutes of deliberate "worry time" every morning or evening.

If you can't do anything about an item, cross it off your list and give yourself permission to stop thinking about it. If you can, then schedule the task according to how urgent it is (remember, just because something is in your field of awareness, it doesn't automatically make it important or urgent. You need to consciously decide on its significance in your life and assign your attention accordingly).

Do this exercise for a week or so and you may start to notice interesting patterns. You might see that you tend to have the very same limited set of worries over and over. You'll see that worrying about such things achieves very little, since the same items remain unchanged whether you worry or not—so you may as well not worry. You may also notice that when you schedule your worries and distractions for a fixed time every day, so much of what seemed very important and urgent a few hours ago suddenly seems much less so. Many issues resolve themselves over time, so there's no point wasting time worrying about them.

Summary:

- In lean, minimalist learning, we identify and focus on the twenty percent of a new task that is genuinely unfamiliar, and deliberately leverage the eighty percent we already have some pre-existing knowledge about.

- Leverage the way your brain already learns by meaningfully connecting new and unusual information to concepts you have already mastered. Start every new lesson with a mind map that captures what you already know, then scan the material to get a high-level overview of how it's organized.

Finally, make deliberately vivid connections and associations between new and old, and revisit your original mind map to track progress.

- Being a minimalist learner is about thoughtful, value-driven, conscious consideration of new information, and a proactive attempt to structure your learning efforts to match. Minimalism often requires decluttering, but it's about the clarity and purpose behind what is removed and what remains, and not about *what* you're choosing to keep. Declutter your learning space, your mindset/attitude, and your routines, processes, and habits. Look at your life and remove what does not directly support your stated learning goals.

- Remember that your attention and awareness are your most valuable resources; you get to choose how you "spend" them. What is the least that needs to happen for you to make concrete progress toward your goal? Take concrete action.

- To minimize information overload, actively engage with new content and reflect on its relevance to your goals and values. Most data we encounter will be irrelevant to us, outdated, inaccurate, inappropriate, or flat out wrong. We need to continually identify what we need to know, how much we need to know, and its deeper value. Develop your informational boundaries. Finally, learn to recognize when information overwhelm is just low self-esteem or fear in disguise.

Chapter 3: Learning to Learn

Whatever you're learning, mindset matters, and so does your overall learning philosophy and strategy. That's because the techniques and approaches you use stem directly from this mindset. In this chapter, we'll be taking a closer look at what actually takes place when we learn day after day, and which handful of techniques and approaches works best across the board.

The Five-Hour Rule

First, the **one resource that is more important than all the others because we can never create more of it: time.**

What makes a day? We all have twenty-four hours, no matter who we are. Biologically, most of us do best at around six to nine hours of sleep a day (leaving nice wide margins) and, if we work full time in a conventional job, may spend a further eight to ten hours at our day jobs. That leaves around seven or eight hours for other things like exercising, socializing, housework, life admin, childcare, relaxation, hobbies, eating, grooming . . . and learning something new.

While that seven or eight hours might seem like a lot, most of us have had the experience of getting to the end of the day and genuinely feeling that we had "no time" to do all those things we wanted to do. The culprit is obvious: You watched TV, you scrolled through your phone, you watched TV again, you checked your email, you pottered around the house, you looked at your phone again . . .

The majority of people have a few hours of free time each day, every day, but many of them waste that time on tasks that achieve precisely nothing. In fact, most of these tasks barely even count as relaxation—when last did an hour on your phone or in front of a TV make you feel refreshed and rejuvenated?

We can find some good advice hidden in the 80/20 rule again: Take a good look at your daily schedule and identify that useless eighty percent that is not moving you toward what you truly value. You may discover that when you are focused, disciplined, and willing to cut away at the nonsense of life, there is *plenty* of time available to work toward your dreams.

Enter the "five-hour rule," which suggests spending one hour per day on learning, reflection, and deep thinking. At the end of a five-day week, you will have accrued five solid hours of quality time—there's that magic twenty percent. In a year, you will have spent more than one thousand hours on high-value tasks. Bearing in mind that a four-year degree can take around four thousand to six thousand hours of classroom time, this is nothing to sniff at, especially when you consider the other, hidden benefit of all the time you're *not* spending on harmful activities. Wouldn't you rather have accumulated one thousand high-value hours than one thousand hours on being a coach potato?

This rule is inspired by Benjamin Franklin, who was said to have dedicated at least an hour each day to learning something new. Franklin prioritized reading and writing and even formed a club of like-minded individuals.

Today, successful figures such as Elon Musk, Oprah Winfrey, and Bill Gates also follow variations of the five-hour rule.

Investing just an hour each day into education stimulates the mind, enhances skills, and cultivates discipline. While it may seem daunting at first, you may soon discover (once you retrain a flagging attention span) that you are more than capable of filling up that hour and may even go over it on some days. However, the very fact that you assign just one hour is itself an exercise in prioritizing—if you have just one hour, you'd better choose something really important, and you'd better tackle it the most efficient way possible!

This approach embodies the principle of "less is more" by emphasizing concentrated effort, deliberate practice, and strategic time allocation. By investing a limited amount of time in deep learning and reflection, individuals can achieve significant growth while still maintaining balance in their lives.

One caveat here is that simply devoting hours to your learning is not enough—you need dedicated time where you're thinking about thinking, learning about learning, reflecting, planning, and contemplating the bigger picture. Think of this hour like the control panel in an aircraft. It's where you sit down and take a reading on everything that's going on, check the course you're on, and make any adjustments.

How Should You Spend Your Hour?
Be Committed, Be Flexible

The first thing to do is simply agree with yourself that the hour a day is really happening, and that's that. Naturally, you'll come up with some reasons (read: excuses) why you can't do that hour, but simply make a promise with yourself that as convincing as these arguments sound, they will make no difference, and you'll do the hour no matter what.

Excuses can even be useful—simply take whatever you believe is standing in your way and find some route around it:

"I can't read at the end of the day; my eyes are so tired by then . . ."

"That's okay! Read in the beginning of the day, or listen to audiobooks."

"The kit is so expensive, though."

"That's okay! Buy it secondhand, or save up and in the meantime find a way to practice without the kit."

"I can't do that because I have to walk the dogs."

"That's okay! You can hire a dogwalker or get someone else to walk the dogs in exchange for another chore you do for them."

If you hear yourself thinking "But I don't have any time," realize that this is really just secret code for "Today I haven't prioritized the thing I said I value."

Experiment

Bettering yourself doesn't have to mean doing a grueling high-level academic course or learning to bungee jump. It doesn't have to mean reading Tolstoy or learning chess just because those are the things you imagine intelligent, evolved people do. You might have a fixed idea of what you're meant to be doing to improve yourself, but don't be afraid to challenge that assumption—what are some *other* ways you can achieve what you want?

Successful people don't get where they are by accident, and they seldom get where they are by mindlessly following what other people did. Sometimes, the biggest thing you have to learn is to let go of your preconceived ideas of what success will look like for *you*, as the unique person you are, with the unique talents and goals you possess.

Try something new. If something isn't working, see what happens if you do it a little differently. Let go of the idea that fun and learning are two different things! If you're feeling fearful or unconfident, try to reframe your tasks so they're not performances or things you have to do perfectly. Rather, see them as interesting games or something you're playing around with and trying out. Try to imagine that there is no wrong move— everything you do yields interesting new information and, with the right mindset, can be learned from.

Reflect

We've seen that there is an optimal attitude to failure (i.e., the state of mind that understands that failure doesn't get in the way of learning—it IS learning). Like Samuel Beckett says, "Try again. Fail again. Fail better." Make your goal to be continually making more sophisticated mistakes as you go along. Failure is part of the process, but it only has value if you can mine it for the lesson it holds—that means not making the same mistake twice.

Reflecting means stepping back to look at your failures and your successes. It's looking at what you've done to bring about those failures and successes, and making a plan for what you'll do next, given that insight. You'll know you've mastered this kind of reflection when you can look at yourself completely neutrally—with no judgment, no shame, no doubt, just curiosity. Some days you might want to just reflect for a full hour; others you may only need five minutes. Use a diary or journal, or just mull over things in your own mind. The way you think about things will make the difference between "failure" and "priceless learning experience."

Running to Stay Still

It's a scary and uncomfortable fact, but **the world is moving at such a pace that every day you simply stay still and fail to learn is actually a day you take a step *backward*.** Everything you know right now is gradually being updated and expanded, so that if you choose to do nothing, that knowledge and expertise will eventually depreciate over time. In other words, acquired skill and learning is not permanently banked—

According to writer Michael Simmons, it takes around a decade for fifty percent of the facts in any study area to be improved on, updated, or completely discarded. That means that in any particular field, half of what appears to be relevant and cutting edge today will be outdated and forgotten within ten years, or even less. A *Harvard Business Review* article claimed that skills and knowledge taught in degree courses today will likely expire in just five years or so.

Simmons did the math and calculated that in just one year's time, around five percent of the knowledge you had about that field would be lost, and in five years about twenty-five percent. If you wanted to counteract this loss, you would need to find time for an additional 250 or 1250 hours of learning, respectively. This, however, would be learning done simply to stay relevant, i.e., running to stay in place.

If that sounds scary, consider that new people coming into the field will be more up-to-date and will be actively spending time training and developing themselves. Plus, we naturally lose some of what we learn through forgetfulness, which means that Simmons's figures are probably on the low side. All in all, the message is clear: Five hours a week is likely the *least* you can do to keep up and stay relevant in your chosen field.

Now, not everyone wants to learn something purely so they can be competitive in a professional capacity. And some skills *are* more timeless and transferable, holding their value for a lot longer than others. That said, it's worth thinking of knowledge itself as having a "half-life" and remembering that it really does make sense to make learning a way of life.

Some things to think about:

What is the ultimate value of the skills and knowledge you're trying to acquire? Even as things change, what remains the same about the core of what you're learning?

What skills, attitudes, and habits are transferable to *any* area of study, and how are you developing them?

Think about innovations in your chosen area of study, and become cautious about the way thought leaders are approaching their learning. What are they focused on, and how do they learn and acquire knowledge? How can you emulate their strategy without copying them?

The Aha! and the Huh?

Maybe your learning goal is to finish a class, course, or eLearning module.

That's great! The trouble is, "finishing a course" is not actually a goal. That's because you can watch all the videos, listen to the recordings, and tick the boxes but not really absorb anything useful. If your goal is to move the little progress bar on the bottom of the screen or win a passing grade on an assignment from a tutor, well, that's fine—but it's not the same as learning, is it?

All of that stuff—processing different multimedia, completing assignments, and so on—is part of the eighty percent, not the twenty percent.

Then what's the twenty percent? Let's keep it really simple: **When you're learning something new, you are essentially having two core experiences—either you're getting something new ("aha!") or you're stumped and don't understand what you're looking at ("huh?").**

It sounds overly simple, but much of your learning comes down to these two states (remember the eighty-five percent rule? We can reformulate it to say that the optimal condition for learning is to be saying "huh?" no more than fifteen percent of the time). As you move through a course of any kind, keep in mind these two key points, and don't get distracted by the format the course is delivered in. For example, your goal is never to "watch three videos" but to actually extract the big idea from each of those videos, understand them, and process them in a way that makes sense for your unique goals.

So, as you learn, whenever an idea "clicks" with you and you have a moment of insight

and understanding, write it down. Try as hard as you can to put things in your own words. Try to capture *why* something has suddenly made sense to you, and what it was that helped you achieve this insight. At the same time, introduce this new piece of information to all your pre-existing knowledge. Connect it to what you know. See what it implies for your goals. These aha! moments may or may not coincide with what the course curriculum is telling you is significant, however.

The other thing is to note when the opposite happens. When you're completely confused and uncomprehending, note this down, too. This part is more important—the way you deal with this point of confusion is crucial for how much you ultimately learn.

Write down questions that you don't have answers to. As best you can, try to identify what you're missing or what doesn't come together for you. Try to find exactly the point at which you lose the thread. Mark it down— you can return to this later when you have figured out the answer (sometimes you just need to be patient and all will be revealed!) or when you need to ask for help or guidance. The great thing about keeping an inventory of snags and issues is that they can act as a baseline, allowing you to see how much you've learned over time. It can be very encouraging to look at tricky questions you had two weeks ago and know that you can confidently resolve them today.

Work on a Running One-Sentence Summary

As you make your way through any new material, get into the habit of establishing a running one-sentence summary of all the new concepts you're learning. In your own words, write a single sentence that summarizes the overall course content to begin with (If you're unsure about this, it's a good sign you need a little more clarity!).

Next, identify some key concepts and quickly establish for yourself a single sentence summary that captures the big idea. For some people, this might look like a Word or Google Doc that acts as a glossary of new terms. Every time you encounter a new word or idea, add it to your glossary with your best understanding of what it means. As you learn, you will return to this glossary and update your definition. Of course, some words will be big "huh?" concepts—that's fine, just note that this is the case and cue yourself to reading actively so that when you find the answer, you are ready to grab it.

Don't worry about this process too much— **you're not aiming for perfection or a finished product, rather you're using these working definitions as a way to keep tabs on your evolving understanding of the key concepts**. Just ask yourself what the word is pointing to, why it exists, and, in plain English, what it means in the broader context. Making summaries right at the end of learning makes less sense—instead, try to build up a condensed and simplified model of what you're learning as you learn it.

The very act of trying to continually extract the most important twenty percent is what is helping you learn, and learn efficiently. When you explain things to yourself in your own language, you have a far greater chance of really grasping and retaining it. When you work for your understanding and insight this way, it's worth much more than simply consuming a pre-made summary someone else has compiled for you.

Reframing things in terms of aha/huh means you approach your learning with a far more engaged, proactive mindset, rather than passively moving through a fixed curriculum in a rote way. Another benefit is that you stop seeing confusion and difficulty as an obstacle. You embrace it and work with it. If you forget something, you go back and consult your original summary list. If you don't get an explanation, you make your own until you grasp the thing that's evading you. Remember that you are not trying to produce a textbook or a set of glossy notes for someone else. Your notes and summaries are for you and are an external representation of your active learning process.

The ADEPT Method

Be glad when you encounter something you don't understand—learn to recognize it as an opportunity for learning. When you're stuck, you might like to use what's called the ADEPT method to help you make that breakthrough in understanding.

ANALOGY—What is it like?

DIAGRAM—How can it be visualized?

EXAMPLE—What does it look like in the real world? Can I experience it myself?

PLAIN ENGLISH—What does it mean in everyday language?

TECHNICAL DEFNITION—What does it mean in specialist, formal terms?

For example, let's say you are learning about the cost function in machine learning, and it's definitely causing a "huh?" reaction. You use the ADEPT method like this:

- **Start with an analogy:** An analogy for the cost function in machine learning can be comparing it to measuring distances on a map. Just like measuring the difference between the actual distance and the predicted distance, the cost function measures the difference between the actual output and the predicted output of a machine-learning model. Sometimes you can get far by describing what a thing *isn't* like, too!

- **Use a diagram:** A diagram representing the cost function can be a graph showing the relationship between the model's parameters and the corresponding cost values. It visually illustrates how adjusting the parameters affects the cost function's shape and helps in understanding optimization processes.

- **Use an example:** Let's say you are working on a machine-learning project to predict housing prices. By applying the cost function to this specific problem, you can calculate the difference between the predicted prices and the actual prices for a set of houses, and iteratively adjust the model's parameters to minimize the cost function and improve the accuracy of predictions. This works even better if you're currently buying or selling a house, or used to work in property sales, because it will speak directly to your experience.

- **Explain in plain and simple language:** To explain the cost function in plain language, you can say that it quantifies how well a machine-learning model is performing by measuring the average difference between its predictions and the actual values. It helps in evaluating and improving the model's accuracy.

- **Convert understanding into technical description:** Once you have a clear understanding of the cost function, you can describe it using mathematical terminology. For example, you can define it as a mathematical expression that calculates the mean squared error between the predicted values and the actual values, incorporating the model's parameters and the training data.

As you can see, it's best to work through the steps in the ADEPT acronym in order, arriving at the end with a more detailed and technical explanation. Though it may seem silly, you can run through this method by pretending you are literally teaching someone else the concept. This will force you to slow down and really find the nub of what you're struggling with—it will also help you test whether you really understand a concept as well as you think you do.

If you get stuck, pretend you're the student and ask questions. "Wait, but why is it the mean *squared* error and not just the mean error?" As you actively lead yourself along to the answer you most need, you are in essence creating your own tailor-made curriculum moment by moment—you are finding that optimal twenty percent path through a pre-existing curriculum, and by navigating that strategic path, you learn faster and more effectively than ever before.

Learning Techniques: What Works, What Doesn't

When learning something new, many people dive in and start to choose their

materials—but it may make more sense to focus on your study methods first.

There are plenty of different study techniques, methods, approaches, and philosophies out there. Which ones genuinely work and which ones should be avoided? Let's apply the 80/20 rules: Of all the possible ways to learn, only around twenty percent of them are going to be responsible for the bulk of good outcomes. It makes sense that we should do what we can to select that twenty percent, rather than just barging ahead with an approach or technique out of habit or just because we don't know what else to do.

Your best bet is to use only those techniques that are evidence-based. Neuroscientists have conducted mountains of research on what the brain actually does when it learns, memorizes, solves problems, etc., and their research can tell us a lot about the learning methods that actually work in tandem with the brain's natural capacities.

The following are some strategies that have been proven to be more effective than the rest, so by implementing them, you are already assured that you can save time, increase efficiency, and maximize the impact of your learning efforts. Rather than investing equal effort across all sorts of different methods, homing in on the most effective ones allows you to prioritize what truly matters and yields the greatest results in terms of knowledge acquisition and skill development.

Take Notes

A 2021 study compared the effectiveness of handwriting and typing for learning. **The researchers found that students who wrote their notes by hand retained information better than those who typed their notes.** Typing seemed to lead to cognitive overload and resulted in lower knowledge retention, accuracy of terminology, and ability to connect ideas. So, when it comes to learning, using pen and paper is more beneficial than typing.

Whatever method you use, some basic tips for notetaking include:

- Listen and take notes in your own words.
- Leave spaces and lines between main ideas so you can revisit them later and add information.
- Develop a consistent system of abbreviations and symbols to save time.
- Write in phrases, not complete sentences.
- Learn to pull out important information and ignore trivial information.

- Add questions, comments, little arrows, or other annotations.
- Use color and symbols to help connect and organize ideas.

Take a Power Nap

Research indicates that taking a nap, around forty-five to sixty minutes, can significantly improve information retrieval from memory. A power nap acts as a reset for the brain, helping to smooth out glitches that occur throughout the day and enhance overall functioning. Author Daniel Pink suggests a caffeine-nap hack, where you drink coffee before taking a twenty-five-minute power nap to coincide with the caffeine's effects. However, the optimal length for a power nap may vary for each person, so it's important to experiment and find the ideal duration for personal effectiveness.

A great idea is to take a nap after an intense learning session, to give your brain time to rest and consolidate—it will literally build new neural connections as you sleep. Another trick is to take a nap when you're stuck. Imagine assigning the problem to your unconscious mind before sleeping; then when you wake up, take a fresh look. You may be surprised at what your mind is capable of when it's "resting."

Spaced Repetition

Spaced repetition involves scheduling repeated reviews of the information to be memorized. This approach is beneficial because we tend to forget a significant portion of what we learn within twenty-four hours . . . unless we review it. Without testing or review, about sixty percent of what we've learned is retained after three days. However, **with each review, memory retention increases**.

For example, let's consider a student studying vocabulary for a foreign language. Instead of cramming all the words in a single study session, they implement spaced repetition. They start by studying a small set of vocabulary words and definitions. The next day, they review and drill the same set of words, along with new ones. They continue this pattern, revisiting the previously learned words while introducing new ones in each study session.

As they progress, the intervals between reviews gradually increase. They might review the words again after a few days, then a week, and eventually after several weeks. With each review, they reinforce their memory of the words and their meanings. The spaced repetition approach allows for more effective long-term retention, as the brain is constantly engaged in refreshing and reinforcing the learned material.

Though spaced repetition makes intuitive sense, a lot of us have study methods that completely ignore it. Remember that comprehension and understanding are *not* the same as remembering—to fix something firmly in the memory, you need to drill it many times over. It makes sense when you think about it; spaced repetition makes you practice the most important thing: recall. The more often you repeat the process of pulling up that stored memory, the easier it becomes. If you leave revision to the last minute, you may find yourself, for example, in an exam situation and trying to recall a fact for the very first time.

ELI5

Theoretical physicist Robert Feynman famously devised a learning method that was all about simplification. **According to Feynman, unless you could explain what you knew to a child, you didn't really understand it as well as you thought you did**. He believed that it was only when you used plain English and straightforward, jargon-free language that you could determine whether you had grasped the deeper underlying concept, rather than just learned to parrot the right words.

He would write the topic on the title page of an empty notebook and then use the "Explain Like I'm Five" (ELI5) technique to break down complex ideas into simpler ones. To apply this technique, take a challenging concept, such as machine learning, and imagine explaining it to a five-year-old using analogies. For example, you could say, "Machine learning is a kind of thinking that a machine can do, where the machine teaches itself without being taught by programmers. The machine looks very quickly through all sorts of information to make a guess about how the world is, but it is also able to look at all its previous guesses and figure out useful lessons from the times it was wrong."

By breaking down complex concepts into smaller, more digestible pieces, you gain a better understanding of how the components fit together (note as well that there is some overlap here with ADEPT analogies).

Another related approach is to write an explanation down that doesn't use any technical language that itself needs further definition. So if you used the term "artificial intelligence" to explain the term "machine learning," does that *really* explain what it is? Try to define "artificial intelligence" without any further jargon, and you will force yourself to grasp the underlying explanatory concepts more quickly. You will force a kind of genuine learning, not just teach yourself to give the outward impression of having learned!

Interleaving

Interleaving is a learning technique where different topics or skills are mixed together instead of focusing on one at a time. This approach has been found to be more effective than learning topics in isolation. For example, when learning to swim, interleaving would involve practicing freestyle, breaststroke, and floating in a mixed pattern, such as alternating between them.

Researchers conducted studies in actual classrooms, where students were assigned interleaved homework assignments that combined algebra and geometry questions. The results showed that after a month, the students who used interleaving performed seventy-six percent better compared to those following the traditional approach of learning one topic at a time.

Implementing interleaving can add variety to your learning process while enhancing retention and understanding. For instance, when learning to code, you can learn CSS, HTML, and JavaScript simultaneously. In management training, you can alternate between people skills, organization skills, and management techniques. If you're learning to draw, for example, you can switch between studying human anatomy, shading techniques, and colors. By interleaving different topics, you can improve your learning outcomes and make the learning experience more engaging.

Creating an Optimal Learning Environment

To create an optimal learning environment, consider the following factors:

Lighting: Natural lighting is preferred, as studies have shown that students perform twenty-five percent better in well-lit environments compared to dim lighting. Position yourself near windows or in areas with access to sunlight for optimal learning conditions.

Colors: Different colors can affect our mood and mindset. Blue promotes calmness, red sparks passion, and yellow fosters positivity and happiness. Identify which colors suit your learning abilities based on your preferences and consult a color psychology guide for further guidance.

Orderliness: A cluttered environment can be distracting and hinder learning. A study from Carnegie Mellon University revealed that students in a clean and organized classroom were less distracted, spent more time focused on tasks, and learned more effectively. Declutter your learning space to optimize your concentration and cognitive abilities.

Mnemonic Devices

Creating a mnemonic is a valuable technique for enhancing memory and retaining information. To make your own mnemonic, start by identifying the specific information or concepts you want to remember. Break down the material into manageable parts and gain a solid understanding of it. Then look for **connections, patterns, or associations between the information and something familiar to you**. Use vivid imagery or visualizations to create mental pictures that link the mnemonic to the information. Personalize the mnemonic by incorporating elements that are meaningful to you. Keep the mnemonic simple and concise to facilitate easy recall. Test and refine the mnemonic through practice to ensure its effectiveness in aiding memory. With practice and customization, mnemonics can become powerful tools for memorization in various areas of learning.

A few fun examples include "My Very Easy Method Just Speeds Up Naming Planets" (helps to remember the order of the planets in the solar system), knowing that "dessert" is spelled with a double s "because you always go back for seconds with desserts," or remembering PEDMAS ("Please Excuse My Dear Aunt Sally") to remember the order of operations in mathematics.

The Memory Palace Technique

This technique is a kind of visual mnemonic, but it is so effective it deserves its own place on the list. Let's say you want to memorize a list of items: pen, apple, book, and key. Using the memory palace technique, you choose your home as your memory palace. Assign each memory item to a place in your home, connecting it via some imagery, emotion, or other cue. Here's how:

- Start at the front door of your home. Visualize a giant pen drawing on the door, leaving colorful marks.
- Move to the living room. Picture a gigantic apple rolling around on the couch, with bites taken out of it.
- Proceed to the kitchen. Imagine a massive book resting on the kitchen counter, open to a page with a recipe for apple pie.

- Finally, head to the bedroom. Envision a giant key hanging from the doorknob, glowing brightly.

By associating each item with a vivid and exaggerated image within a specific location in your memory palace, you create memorable connections. When you mentally walk through your home, you can easily recall the items and their order: pen at the front door, apple in the living room, book in the kitchen, and key in the bedroom. The potential is enormous: You will never forget the layout of your home and, if you make the associations vivid enough, you can recall vast amounts of information with seemingly no effort at all. You may even be able to recall that information years later.

Use   Brain   Breaks

Stress and overwhelm can cause our brains to shut down, leading to decreased focus and learning. To combat this, it is crucial to **incorporate brain breaks and restorative activities into our learning routine.**

One effective way to give your brain a break is through meditation. Taking just a few minutes to engage in meditation practice can help calm the mind, reduce stress, and enhance focus and concentration. Another option is to use essential oils, take a hot bath, or do some relaxing stretching exercises. Going for a walk or implementing a time-blocking system for scheduled breaks can help you recharge and refocus.

By incorporating these restorative activities into your learning routine, you can alleviate brain fatigue, enhance relaxation, and create an optimal environment for effective learning. The big idea, however, is to genuinely "turn your brain off"—there's no point using that time to stress about what work you have to return to!

The Protégé Effect

We've already seen why teaching others can be such an effective way to learn—it helps us slow down, uncover blind spots, and really dig into the core concepts we need to understand.

Research shows that even the expectation of teaching someone else boosts learning effectiveness. By shifting your mindset to focus on sharing knowledge rather than just passing a test, you externalize the material and engage with it on a deeper level. Anticipate potential questions that others might ask and seek out answers to those questions. Engage in a realistic simulation where you pretend to teach the material, visualizing the experience and even speaking aloud.

Distributed Practice

Distributed practice involves spreading out multiple study sessions over time to enhance learning—you spend the same amount of total time studying, but you get more out of it. Instead of suggesting we cram information into one long study session, this approach encourages short, spaced-out sessions for more effective and meaningful learning. This gives more time to rest, process, and consolidate what is learned, but it also provides a built-in opportunity for spaced repetition practice.

Start by taking comprehensive notes during discussions or lectures, for example. After each session, spend a few minutes reviewing and refining your notes for accuracy and detail. Initially, aim to review your notes once or twice after each class. As you progress, gradually increase the spacing between study sessions, starting with daily reviews and eventually transitioning to three times a week.

Before we conclude, what *doesn't* work at improving your memory or understanding? One big thing is simply reading through a textbook. Highlighting mindlessly doesn't help much either, unless you use those highlights to compile a summary in your own words for later revision. Instead try active reading, where you engage with the material and scribble notes and questions in the margins.

Set Your Own Learning Standard

When you were at school or college, it was your teachers and lecturers who decided when you had "passed"—and whether or not you had made sufficient progress. They were the ones who acted as the gatekeepers to learning—and consequently you had to figure out how to do whatever they wanted so you could pass through that gate!

But being a self-directed adult learner is different. Who are the arbiters of your learning now?

Is it your professional peers?
Your competitors?
The leaders of your chosen field?
Your future employers?
Your parents?
All those people who said you wouldn't amount to anything?

Actually, the only one who decides whether you've "passed" as an adult learner is *you*.

In a conventional educational setting, "learning standards" are concise and clearly stated descriptions of what students should know and be capable of at a particular stage in their education. They provide guidance for educators in designing lessons and instructional strategies. Teachers are constantly trying to find ways to appraise and rank students without losing sight of their deeper understanding and development—things that are notoriously hard to quantify.

The first thing to know as a self-directed learner is that you are in charge of your learning. That means that you get to choose your own learning standards, too. This can be an empowering and clarifying step because you are both student and teacher—it's up to you to set your own goals and aspirations, to define what you want to achieve and how you want to achieve it, and exactly what learning means to **you**.

On the other side of that empowerment, however, is responsibility: Because you are the only one in charge, you need to take ownership of *all* parts of your learning journey, and that includes being tough on yourself when it's required! Nobody can do the work for you when it comes to homing in on your values, principles, and the promise you make to yourself. Nobody can tell you whether a goal is too easy. Nobody can step in and tell you that you need to tighten up your self-discipline.

This can be tricky at first since for most of us, our earliest educational experiences were always out of our control, and we may have internalized the idea that learning and education are things we do for external reasons, to meet external standards. But relying on external indicators and standardized assessments may not inspire depth understanding of a subject, and it's tempting to confuse the *marker of the goal* and the *goal itself.* For example, you might consider finishing a book, a sign that you have completed your goal, but really, the goal was not to get to the last page, but to absorb and apply the material you found in the book.

If you set poor, confusing, unambitious, or second-hand standards for yourself, you can impair your learning. You can start to focus on the wrong thing. Using someone else's criteria, or not even having criteria in the first place, you start to master all the admin that comes with the learning process, rather than learning itself.

The 80/20 rule can help here. **Ask yourself what the crucial twenty percent is when it comes to demonstrating that you have actually learned new knowledge and mastered new skills**. There are no ready-made checklists for this—you have to reflect on your own and decide what signs and indicators you can use to help you conclude that learning has indeed taken place. A few targeted questions can help, though:

What are your life values and the principles you like to live by? Can these inspire some of your learning goals and standards? For example, you might decide that you value individuality and authenticity. This makes you decide that you're not learning a new craft just to mimic the masters, but to expand the medium and use it to express your own, totally original ideas.

Think about someone who has already mastered the skill you're trying to master. What are the concrete actions that they do with ease? Focusing on ACTION is a great way to narrow in on what actually matters. Goals and standards that are vague and abstract are less valuable than ones that are actionable and very easy to see at play in the real world. Focus on those.

Consider your ideal ratio of confidence to bravery. Being a beginner is always a little scary—starting out new always entails a little risk of failure or embarrassment. You don't want to launch into big challenges when you're genuinely not ready and dent your confidence, but at the same time, you don't want to wait around until you feel perfectly invulnerable and capable—that day won't come. So decide for yourself at what point you are ready to break out of your comfort zone and take a leap of faith. New tasks should scare you, but not to a debilitating degree. Look within and be honest about where this threshold is for you, and identify a comfortable but generative level of challenge.

Create Your Own Learning Philosophy

If you are forcing yourself to read a lot of complicated pop science about quantum mechanics because you think it will improve your life somehow, forget it—you may benefit more by exploring the *mindset and philosophy* behind the minds who created those theories in the first place. Don't merely memorize the intellectual products of great innovators who have come before you. Instead, look at *how* they were able to innovate, and see what that means for your life. **In other words, don't just swallow someone else's learning experience, but create your own.**

Great physicists like Einstein, Feynman, Rutherford, and Bohr did *not* embark on their life's work because they wanted to be famous, make money, or inflate their egos. Instead, each of these intellectual titans plotted their own utterly unique path to wisdom and mastery, and they did so far beyond the superficial level. Einstein claimed that "the only real valuable thing is intuition. The intellect has little to do on the road to discovery" and "the greatest thing we can experience is the mysterious." Feynman said, "nature's imagination far surpasses our own." Newton claimed that "I do not know what I may appear to the world; but to myself I seem to have been only like a boy playing on the sea-shore, and diverting myself in now and then finding a smoother pebble or a prettier shell than ordinary, whilst the great ocean of truth lay all undiscovered before me."

These are not the voices of people who have let others set the tone and standard of their learning. Rather, these are people who are engaging with learning on the deepest, most profound level—learning for its own sake, learning because it is a beautiful thing with its own irreducible, absolute value, and because they are madly curious about life in all its dazzling complexity and are seeking truth and the joy of engaging with that truth. *That* is something that cannot be captured in an exam grade or a set of bullet points on a marking rubric!

What is your learning philosophy?

Quotes from great people can spark something inside us, but try to capture for yourself the deepest reason and purpose behind your quest to learn, grow, and acquire mastery. Set the bar high for yourself! Make a code and stick to it. These questions can help you further finetune your own guiding principles on your educational journey.

- Do I have a visceral, ingrained analogy about this concept? Can it help me solve problems?
- Can I explain the concept to others? Have I really understood the difference between the thing and the symbol for the thing?
- Will I remember the essential idea after a few months or years?
- Have I merely memorized this content or have I understood it?
- Can I find something to enjoy in the topic? Will I return after I inevitably forget ninety-five percent of it?
- Does this concept actually connect in any meaningful way to my life?

- Am I challenging myself enough?
- Am I waiting for someone else to give me permission to do more/go further?
- Am I making qualitative changes and not just adding on to my learning quantitatively?
- By what metric will I consider my development?

Let's say someone has made the commitment to retrain as a doctor. They set a big list of increasingly difficult goals that all culminate in them being able to graduate from their chosen course with a qualification, register with all the relevant professional bodies, and start to offer their specialist services in the clearly defined manner they've been taught.

But somewhere in this arduous process, they may get so carried away with writing essays, completing practicals, working with supervisors, adhering to professional standards, and ticking all the right boxes, that they forget *why* they are doing any of it in the first place. When they stop and reflect, they remind themselves of what all this learning is really for, and understand that it means nothing until they absorb it, pass it through their own system of values, and apply it in a meaningful way. The grades and qualifications they receive are like training wheels. The real heart of their learning goes far beyond this and kicks into place when the training wheels come off.

A good med student might realize what the greater, overarching learning standard is: to be an agent of good and to use the very best tools to reduce suffering in the world. If a student constantly has *this* as their ultimate educational standard, they will always be a more effective, more sophisticated learner than the student whose goal is merely to "be top of the class."

Summary:

- Your learning mindset matters because it determines your overall philosophy and approach and the techniques you use.
- Time is the most important resource, so be mindful of how you use it. The "five-hour rule" encourages us not to waste precious time on irrelevant activities, but spend at least an hour a day on meta-learning, reflection, and deep thinking. Commit to that hour and experiment with how you use it. Realize that the world is moving at such a pace that you need to learn continually just to stay relevant.

- Don't get distracted by the format of new material, but just focus on whether you're learning something new ("aha!") or you're stumped ("huh?"). Note down every "aha!" and "huh?" moment and work with them directly. Simultaneously get into the habit of creating a running one-sentence summary of all the new concepts you're learning. For difficult concepts, use the ADEPT method to increase understanding: For each concept find an analogy, diagram, example, plain English, and technical definition, in that order.

- Only twenty percent of study methods will yield eighty percent of your results, so use evidence-based approaches like active reading and notetaking, spaced repetition, distributed practice, interleaving, regular breaks, and mnemonic devices such as the "memory palace technique."

- When you are a self-directed learner, you create your own learning standards and your own learning philosophy, rather than looking to external standards to tell you what to value and why. Set your own goals and measure them by your own metrics. This makes you a more effective, sophisticated, and resilient learner.

Chapter 4: The 80/20 Rule Can Solve Problems

The 80/20 rule can help you identify what goals are most important, what tasks are most likely to get you there, and what mindset you need to adopt if you hope to do those tasks to the very best of your ability. This rule really is *everywhere* and will constantly remind you to keep things lean, don't get distracted by trivial details, and regularly check in with the core of what you're trying to learn and why you're trying to learn it.

You already know you need to have rock-solid goals and a learning philosophy that's all your own. Once those are in place, you can then **reframe any snags and obstacles in your journey as opportunities to check up on**

your strategy overall. The 80/20 principle can help us find useful answers to the question: is what we're doing working?

The Pareto principle can help you decide. The rule suggests that roughly eighty percent of our outcomes will come from twenty percent of our efforts, which means if we want to be more effective, we need to identify the techniques and exercises that are bringing the greatest results, and focus on those.

How to Evaluate Your Learning Experiences
When you've completed a learning task, a course, or some other project, your initial reaction might be relief—phew, you're done! Time for a break.

But you're not done yet! **The learning process continues even after you've reached your deadlines, written your exams, or met your goal. You need to evaluate the process itself. This allows you to "learn how to learn."**

If I ask you "How was your learning process?" how would you answer?

If you ask a school kid what they think of fifth grade or of math class, they may give answers like,

"I hate my teacher."

"The book is so boring."

"I don't see why we have to learn geometry at all!"

"I got a B on the quiz."

But each of these answers is only really addressing a very small part of the learning process. They may tell you a little about the practical way the material was delivered, but they don't say much about how well it's been absorbed, or why or how. Similarly, if you complete an online course and the only reaction you have to it is that you didn't like the platform or the tutor's voice, you've missed out on an opportunity to gain real insight into your learning process.

By observing and reflecting on your learning experiences, you can refine your study strategies and allocate your time and effort more efficiently. But doing this requires more than simply saying "I liked it" or "I passed." Evaluating your learning requires more discernment and self-awareness so you can optimize your learning process, focus on the most productive techniques, and ultimately achieve better results in your learning journey.

To do this, try the Kirkpatrick Model, which was developed by Donald Kirkpatrick in 1954 and has ever since been a popular method for evaluating the effectiveness of training programs, eLearning courses, and other educational initiatives. In fact the creator of the model later became a professor at the University of Wisconsin and the president of the American Society for Training and Development. The model is usually used for people designing and marketing courses and educational materials, but it's a great framework for analyzing self-directed learning, too, and helps you decide on the quality and usefulness of certain educational paths. The model consists of four criteria: **reaction, learning, behavior, and results**. Let's take a closer look.

Level 1 Evaluation—Reaction

This level focuses on gauging your reactions to the learning material. It involves gathering feedback to determine if you enjoyed the experience and found the material useful— this is akin to a school kid saying they like their teacher because she's funny or they dislike the book because it's boring. It's an important (although admittedly nonessential) part of the learning process.

Ask yourself questions like:

- Did I enjoy the learning program?
- What's my opinion on the overall theoretical approach taken?
- How did the material actually make me feel?
- Did I find the material useful and relevant to my needs?
- Did the learning material engage me and keep my interest?

- **Pareto question**: Which part of the course was *most* enjoyable? How can I bring more of that into my learning?

Based on your answers, you can determine if your initial reaction was positive or negative and if there are any areas for improvement or feedback to provide. Of course, not every learning path needs to be easy or entertaining, but it should ideally be engrossing and interesting and rouse overall positive feelings, like curiosity.

Level 2 Evaluation—Learning
This level assesses the new skills, knowledge, or attitudes you've acquired by taking the approach you have. It involves evaluating what you've learned . . . and being honest about what you haven't. Saying "I got an A" is one way to evaluate how well you've learned, but there's far more to it.

To fully evaluate the extent of your learning, consider the following questions:

- What specific new skills, knowledge, or attitudes have I acquired through the material?
- Have I developed other intangible skills, like resilience or discipline?
- How do I compare to others in my peer group?
- Of all the information I took in, how much have I actually absorbed?
- How am I performing on standardized tests? What does this mean to me?
- Can I confidently *apply* what I've learned in real-life situations?
- Are there any areas where I feel I still need improvement or further practice?

- **Pareto question:** What has been the single *biggest and most useful* skill I've learned?

The key here is that you are evaluating—not judging. Shame or blame is unnecessary and can get in the way. Instead, you're simply appraising the effectiveness of your approach in a neutral, curious way. Try to maintain absolute confidence in your own worth and value—but absolute skepticism when it comes to your method.

Level 3 Evaluation—Transfer

Are you able to apply the skills you've learned outside of the narrow realm in which you've learned them? Learning is not just about knowledge; it's about expanding capability and competence. You want to be able to take a new mindset, problem-solving ability, attitude, or set of behaviors and apply it to other areas of life. When school kids complain that they have to do trigonometry even though they can't see how it will ever relate to their real lives, they have a point!

Ask yourself:

- What broader transferable skills have I developed?
- If I can't see the applicability of this new material, is it because it genuinely *isn't* useful, or simply because I haven't yet understood the way it can be applied elsewhere?
- Have I been actively finding ways to connect these skills to real life? If not, how could I do so?
- Can I identify specific instances or examples where I have utilized what I learned?
- Have there been any observable changes in my behavior or performance as a result of the learning process?

- **Pareto question:** Of everything I've learned, what is the most versatile and universally useful twenty percent?

Bearing in mind that though learning sometimes feels like an invisible, inward process, it always manifests externally in changed behavior and concrete action in the real world. Evaluating the way your *total behavior* changes in the real world is a great way to evaluate the effectiveness of a study program.

Level 4 Evaluation—Results

This level focuses on measuring the *overall impact* and results of the learning program. Saying "I passed the test" is one way to evaluate outcomes, but also become curious about why you passed and how you did it. Remember that external standards of success are only there as guidelines—always be curious about what they're intending to measure, and confirm that you have actually met these standards.

- Have I observed any positive changes in my work or daily life as a result of my learning?
- What is my performance like compared to the goals I initially set for myself?
- Can I quantify any tangible benefits or improvements linked to the learning?

- Are there any specific goals or targets that have been achieved due to the learning?

- **Pareto question:** In five years' time, what will I say was the single *most impactful* outcome of this course of learning?

While these questions may seem quite obvious, the truth is that we can often become so caught up in the learning process itself that we fail to stop and appraise how far we've come, what we've achieved, and what still remains to be conquered. But if we don't do that, we don't give ourselves the opportunity to make small course corrections along the way, to adapt and adjust as we go, and to quickly drop things that just aren't working.

Once you've asked all the above questions and reflected on your answers, don't just leave it at that. Internalize what you've learned from the reflection process itself and use this to make adjustments to your learning, whichever stage you're at. The goal of this evaluation is to take charge of your role as your own guru, mentor, and teacher.

Establishing a very clear connection between your learning choices and outcomes keeps you focused and honest. Beyond that, it also gives you something to celebrate. If you have made progress, take the time to properly acknowledge the fact and give yourself credit—you've come a long way!

Before we move on, let's consider how this evaluative approach might work in real life. Imagine that you are a competitive showjumper and have committed to daily lessons to improve your technique in preparation for a big national competition. The riding lessons are expensive, so after a month you want to evaluate how well they're going before you commit to more.

The thing is, you strongly dislike the trainer and find their methods quite exhausting. Basically, when evaluating the first aspect, reaction, your emotional response is pretty negative. However, when you consider the other aspects, a different picture emerges.

When you look at how much you're learning, you realize you're making advances extremely quickly. When you consider the applicability of what you're learning and its transfer to other areas of life, you actually notice that other things have improved for you too: You're more assertive in everyday life, you're more disciplined, and your lifestyle is healthier.

Finally, you do the big competition and place higher than you even dreamed of—success! By running this evaluation, you realize that it's a great idea to continue weekly lessons with this trainer. If you had only done an incomplete evaluation (for example, "The trainer is way too die-hard. I don't like him at all. I'm quitting!"), then you would have missed out on a real learning opportunity.

Overcoming Learning Plateaus

When you're learning something new, it's a given that at some point, you're going to hit a wall. If learning takes place outside of your comfort zone, then this implies that learning is sometimes pretty uncomfortable! But the 80/20 rule can help us out once again and can be applied to help us break through this wall, overcome setbacks and challenges, and work through problems so that we come out on the other end stronger and smarter.

A learning plateau might be one of the most annoying things in the world. You may feel fired up and excited. You're making progress, you're getting better, and then all of a sudden . . . it comes to a screeching halt. You start to feel like you can't go any further. Any new endeavor tends to come with a few "easy gains" to start with. We can travel far on our own natural capacities and the initial excitement of embarking on that new path. But what happens when the excitement has worn off a little and we are reaching the end of those easy gains?

Beware the plateau because it's actually one of your biggest learning opportunities, but in disguise.

If you start to feel yourself flatlining, you may slowly become complacent and stop pushing yourself. The feeling of learning and growing (having those "aha!" moments) becomes less and less frequent until the whole idea starts to feel alien to you.

Anders Ericsson and Robert Pool, authors of *Peak: Secrets from the New Science of Expertise*, say that

> "When you first start learning something new, it is normal to see rapid—or at least steady—improvement, and when that improvement stops, it is natural to believe you've hit some sort of implacable limit. So you stop trying to move forward, and you settle down to life on that plateau. This is the major reason that people in every area stop improving."

This is bad news because it may set up a self-fulfilling prophecy. Your brain adapts to the situation, so that it becomes less able to cope with challenge and novelty over time ... which leads to you seeking out even less challenge and novelty.

To break out of this vicious cycle, you only need to do one thing: Expose yourself to new stimuli, take courageous action, and get moving again!

The 80/20 rule tells us, however, that just twenty percent of our possible actions will help shift a plateau, whereas eighty percent of them will be much less effective. The problem is that the twenty percent actions are usually the ones we're most afraid of.

You may push yourself and fail, so you hang back and choose the eighty percent task instead. Unfortunately, breaking through a plateau usually requires failing! The solution is not to try to avoid that failure, but to embrace it and push through—that's the secret doorway that will take you to the next level.

Advancing in this way means you have to be brave and put at risk all that you've achieved so far. It feels so good to learn and grow and gather achievements. Why would you want to push forward and feel like an unsure, embarrassed beginner again? This speaks to an aspect of human psychology called "loss aversion"—we are sometimes more driven by fear and the attempt to avoid losing something than we are by ambition and hope and the attempt to gain something additional. But loss aversion is part of a mindset that will keep you stuck at a plateau.

Embracing Discomfort

There is an irony in learning. We embark on it because we want to know, and we want the sense of empowerment and mastery that comes with understanding. And yet, on our path to learning, we are very frequently challenged to embrace the fact that we don't know, that we cannot do something, that we are not yet in control. It's the old catch-22: you cannot improve something unless you are willing to acknowledge fully that it's not perfect as it is. You cannot find insight until you are ready to fully inhabit your current position of ignorance—and move through it.

If you have already made some advances on your learning journey, you may have achieved a certain level that is somewhat workable, and you're comfortable with that. You're not an expert or anything, but you can get by. **This**

may feel like success, but this very comfort and contentment with your lot may also be a kind of trap. Why bother taking on the discomfort of tackling the next level when you can just sit back and enjoy being moderately accomplished on a lower level, right?

Thus, a plateau might be a genuine limit to your abilities, but it's more often about your *subjective belief* in that limit.

Growth comes at those points when we're most scared, most resistant, and least sure of ourselves. Growth happens, in other words, at the plateaus! Our attitude determines whether this is our new normal forever, or whether it can become a potential inflection point to continue improving.

To bust through a plateau, reframe what is happening:

Embrace the challenge and scariness.

Look at what you're avoiding and turn to face it full-on instead.

Be okay with failing—in fact, anticipate it and be prepared to extract maximum insight when it happens.

Here are some step-by-step suggestions if you're feeling you've stalled.

Step 1: Identify the Big Thing you're avoiding

What challenge is waiting for you on the horizon? Have you been pulling back from it?

Perhaps you've spent ages practicing an instrument but are too nervous to actually make the leap to perform in front of others. Maybe you've qualified or earned a new certificate but are not feeling confident enough to go out there and start using those new skills. Or maybe there's an optional test that will allow you access to the next level, but you're hesitating because you're not sure if you're truly ready.

Keep your focus on exactly what this Big Thing is—it holds the key to the way out of your plateau. Decide with yourself that you *won't* be taking baby steps toward that goal, but rather be opting for big, bold action.

It may make it easier to simply come to terms with the fact that it will be uncomfortable. Some people de-catastrophize the process by assuming that it will be awkward and uncomfortable. If they can laugh at themselves or even deliberately court that awkwardness, it's over all the more quickly and they can just get on with moving forward.

So perhaps you just dive in and sign up to an open mic in a few days, or put your name down to do the optional test before you have the chance to argue with yourself or come up with excuses. Sometimes, the thing we're most afraid of is something that's already happened and we're afraid it will happen again. But the only way to remove the power of that next step is to tackle it head-on. Think of it this way: Your learning is on the other side of a few uncomfortable experiences, so why not get those experiences out of the way as soon as possible?

Step 2: Refresh your technique

You may have an approach what works. That's great. But remind yourself that the skills you currently possess are only good at getting you to where you currently are—they are clearly *not* good at getting you beyond that point; otherwise you wouldn't be at a plateau.

So, bank those skills, but become curious about what additional techniques might start to work for you. Think about the many different *ways* you can achieve what you're trying to achieve, and the different paths to get there. Here's Anders Ericsson again:

> "The best way to move beyond [a plateau] is to challenge your brain or your body in a new way. Bodybuilders, for instance, will change the types of exercises they are doing, increase or decrease the weight they're lifting or the number of repetitions, and switch up their weekly routine. Actually, most of them will vary their patterns proactively so they don't get stuck on plateaus in the first place."

Switch things up so you don't get too complacent, but also so that you are regularly exposing yourself to new ways to be effective. You will be training yourself to never become too reliant on a single way of doing things. You'll notice this aligns well with the technique of "interleaving." Take a look at the weakest part of your current approach and try to shake things up. See where eighty percent of your mistakes are coming from, and target that. You won't improve by continually doing the same thing.

For example, you may be working really hard on a creative writing course, and sitting down to write every day without fail. You may have read all the right books and done all the right exercises, and your effort has paid off because you really have improved in your writing technique. But if you've hit a plateau, it may be a sign that it's time to do something different. Join a writer's group where you start sharing your work with others, actively seeking their feedback (you might be tackling a Big Thing challenge at the same time!). Start to submit some of your work to magazines and other publications, or enter competitions. Hire a writing coach and set some new goals. You can continue to write every day and do your creative writing course, but you're opening up to new avenues through which your learning can come.

Step 3: Go bigger

Sometimes you can break through a plateau simply by committing to taking on bigger challenges. Human beings tend to want to take the path of least resistance. You need to consistently challenge yourself to do a little more, whether that's mentally, emotionally, or physically, to counteract the natural human tendency to be somewhat risk-averse and conservative (in a word, lazy!).

If you suspect you might be underchallenging yourself, it may be time for a BHAG—that's a big, hairy, audacious goal! The term comes from authors Jim Collins and Jerry Porras in their book, *Built to Last: Successful Habits of Visionary Companies*. They explain how a BHAG is compelling, long-term, intriguing, inspiring, a little scary . . . and BIG! They're what you need when your motivation is flagging a little or when you've lost big-picture thinking about your life in general, and where your goals fit into a broader vision. A BHAG should excite you and scare you a little. It should feel almost out of reach, but tantalizing in a way that makes you think, "But what if I *could* actually do that . . .?"

To make your own BHAG, set a goal that makes you say a resounding yes to the following questions:

- Does it really stimulate and excite you?
- Does it feel thrilling and adventurous?
- Is it something you can honestly envision throwing your whole self into?
- Would it be simply amazing if you achieved it?

Too many of us dream small because we think it's prudent to be cautious. But sometimes this sentiment also comes from a lack of self-belief and plain old fear. What happens next is that we establish a feedback loop where every twinge of discomfort or doubt confirms for us the idea that we are going too far, wanting too much, or stepping out of our place.

But discomfort and awkwardness are *not* a sign that something is wrong, or that you should quit. Your goal is *not* to create a life that is as easy and comfortable as possible! Your goal is to grow and learn. Get into the habit of asking whether you can actually dial up your goals by twenty percent. You may discover that you are unnecessarily limiting yourself and are stronger than you give yourself credit for.

Okay, so you're scared about committing to that fun run on the weekend. But instead of putting it off till next year, go one step further—do the fun run *and* commit to the full marathon in three months' time. Now focus on how amazing you're going to feel when you cross that finish line and prove to yourself just how much you're capable of.

Problem-Solving with Pareto Analysis

What is your usual technique for dealing with problems when they arise?

Most people don't have an answer to this question because they secretly hope that they never do encounter problems, and if they do, their strategy for dealing with it is something like "Do whatever you can to avoid it as much possible, I guess?"

If you're interested in doing things well, you need to be interested in all the many ways that you can do them *poorly*, too. In other words, truly mastering a new skill or having a depth understanding of certain concepts require you to actively manage the failing part as well as the succeeding part—with the right mindset, these are just two sides of the same coin, both yielding interesting, actionable data that helps you improve next time.

Using the Pareto principle, we can say that when we have difficulty mastering challenging material or tasks, eighty percent of this difficulty will be coming from just twenty percent of the problems. So, if we're struggling with an instrument, a language, a sport, or a complex scientific problem, we can often nail down our struggle to a small number of very impactful problems, such as incorrect technique holding the instrument, fundamentally misunderstanding the most commonly used tense, basic hand-eye coordination, and a foundational understanding of the scientific concepts you're taking as given.

So far we've used the Pareto principle to help us identify the mindsets, actions, and techniques that are most impactful. In this final chapter, we'll turn that on its head and try to identify the twenty percent of problems, failures, and misunderstandings that are causing us the most trouble. Putting this very simply, we can say that the 80/20 rule for problem-solving is: **solve the biggest and most impactful problems first.**

You can guess what the next question is: How do you identify precisely which problem is the biggest or most impactful? If you're finding everything confusing, how on earth can you identify which points of confusion will yield the most insight if you were to work to untangle them?

Enter "Pareto analysis," which allows us to systematically observe our problems and note the frequency of their occurrence. When you're confused and finding things hard, you might not even know why or in what way you're struggling . . . but you can definitely become curious about what type of problem keeps popping up again and again. If twenty percent of the causes are behind eighty percent of the problems you are able to witness, then solving that twenty percent instantly improves the majority of your outcomes. It's like finding the main roots of a weed and cutting them, rather than wasting time trimming its many branches and offshoots.

However, to do this requires an initial mindset shift. Our ordinary tendency is to think of problems as something annoying, unexpected, unfair, and worthy of being avoided and moved on from as quickly as possible. Turn this on its head: **Face problems as something valuable, totally expected, unavoidable, neutral, and requiring your undivided attention and interest**. Be grateful for problems and consider them especially valuable teachers. The irony is that approaching problems this way is the only real way to get rid of them. Trying to avoid or ignore inevitable difficulties and issues simply guarantees that you'll be stuck with those issues for a very long time!

Not all problems are created equal. The most impactful problem will also tend to be the scariest, the most complicated, and the most uncomfortable to deal with. That means that many people consciously or unconsciously hold off on addressing the biggest issue in their learning process, choosing instead to waste time on solving "eighty percent problems" that were having only a negligible impact on overall performance, anyway. But think of it this way: If you only have a limited amount of time, energy, and resources to dedicate to problem-solving, it's wise to spend that on the biggest cause. Choosing the easy and obvious problems first seems preferable, but actually just wastes your time and leaves you with less of it with which to tackle the real issue.

If you're having trouble in your learning process, relax, take a deep breath, and confirm for yourself in your mind that this is exactly what learning *is*—don't give up and don't try to escape the issues. Then, try the following:

Step 1: Identify all the problems you're currently having and put them in a table. This alone may take some time, but you are looking for cause-effect relationships. When you have a problem, stop and try to capture what went wrong in a sentence and put it on your table. Continue doing this until you've gathered plenty of data. When you notice the same kind of problem emerging, note this on your table so that you're keeping a running tally of how often you're encountering this sort of hiccup.

Step 2: Rank the problems. To begin identifying which issues in this list are the most important twenty percent, simply look at which problems are occurring most frequently. When you're done gathering data, put the problems in order from most to least frequently occurring.

Step 3: Analyze your data. Add up the total number of problems you've observed—let's say for ease it's one hundred. Now you can calculate the relative contribution of each problem as a percentage. For example, you can note that forty percent of all your troubles are caused by just one main issue. You may wish to tweak the data a little depending on the nature of your problems. But in the end, you should have a clear picture of exactly what you need to focus on—look for the problem that is causing the most trouble and try to solve it first.

Let's look at an example.

Imagine you're a beginner and learning how to code, but you find yourself overwhelmed with all the new concepts, terms, and tools. You want to prioritize your learning efforts by identifying the most significant areas that will provide the highest impact in your coding journey. All you have to work with, however, are lots and lots of problems. Lucky you!

To apply Pareto analysis in this scenario, you would start by collecting data on the challenges and difficulties you encounter while learning to code. These challenges could include understanding basic syntax, grasping fundamental programming concepts, struggling with logical thinking, or facing difficulties with debugging code. Whatever snag you encounter, you note it down in a spreadsheet that you keep for a week.

As you progress in your coding journey, you accumulate multiple occurrences of these challenges, noting their frequency. Once you have enough data, you put this data in visual form, perhaps as a pie chart or bar graph, to really drive home that it is just one or two big issues causing your sense of confusion.

For example, you might find that *struggling with logical thinking* is the most significant cause that impacts your progress in understanding programming concepts and writing code effectively. With this insight, you can now prioritize your learning efforts accordingly. Instead of attempting to tackle every concept and language equally, you can focus on the vital few areas that contribute to the majority of your challenges. In this case, you would dedicate more time and effort to improving your logical thinking skills as they manifest in each emerging problem. You already know that chances are high that you're struggling because of this cause, so you can ask yourself, "What is going wrong with my logical thinking right now? How can I improve this one aspect as it relates to the problem in front of me?"

By utilizing Pareto analysis, you avoid wasting time on less significant challenges and instead focus on the most critical aspects of coding. This approach helps you make informed decisions about where to allocate your learning efforts, leading to more efficient progress and skill development. But it also has the happy side effect of reducing overwhelm. What starts out feeling like a confusing and chaotic mess starts to seem far more manageable.

In fact, using Pareto analysis can also help you identify core concepts in general (each occurrence of a problem is a "huh?" moment that can shape your learning journey). When you return to this material later to review it, you will find you're already halfway to compiling a summary of core concepts. In other words, **the twenty percent most impactful problems tend to align very closely with the twenty percent most important key concepts overall.**

Pareto analysis can be applied to all sorts of problems. Here's how it might look if you're learning to draw and paint but are having trouble. After a week or two you have:

- **Problem 1:** Difficulty with proportion and perspective (4)
- **Problem 2:** Challenges in shading and creating realistic values (9)
- **Problem 3:** Lack of understanding of anatomy and proportions (10)
- **Problem 4:** Trouble with capturing accurate details and textures (2)

You then arrange the problems from highest to lowest based on the number of occurrences.

- **Problem 3:** Lack of understanding of anatomy and proportions (10)
- **Problem 2:** Challenges in shading and creating realistic values (9)

- **Problem 1:** Difficulty with proportion and perspective (4)
- **Problem 4:** Trouble with capturing accurate details and textures (2)

You then study the data and decide what to prioritize. There are four identified problems, but the analysis reveals that problems 3 and 2 should be resolved first to achieve the most impact. Working on problems 1 and 4 instead would yield minimal results. However, it's important to note that this analysis doesn't discount the significance of the other problems; it simply helps prioritize them.

Summary:

- The 80/20 principle can help us solve problems efficiently and find useful answers to the question: is what we're doing working? We can reframe any snags and obstacles in the learning journey as opportunities to check up on your strategy overall.
- The learning process continues even after you've reached your deadlines, written your exams, or met your goal. Evaluate the learning process itself so you can make useful adjustments and learn how to learn.

By observing and reflecting on your learning experiences, you can refine your study strategies and allocate your time and effort more efficiently.

- One way is to use the Kirkpatrick Model and analyze on four levels: initial reaction (how enjoyable you found it), learning (what you actually learned), transfer (how applicable the learning is more broadly), and results (what the outcome is compared against goals).

- When we hit a plateau and our learning stagnates, it's important to identify the twenty percent actions that will get us moving again—they're usually the scariest ones. Breaking through plateaus requires us to expose ourselves to new stimuli, take courageous action, and get moving again.

- To keep learning and developing, embrace discomfort and don't get complacent in gains you've already made and banked. Identify the Big Thing you're avoiding and tackle it head-on, switch up your technique and try something new, or push yourself to commit to a bigger and more ambitious goal.

- The Pareto principle can help us become efficient problem-solvers if we understand that eighty percent of our difficulty will come from just twenty percent of problems. Identify your problems, rank them by frequency, and solve the most frequent and impactful ones first. See problems as teachers; expect and welcome their lessons.

Summary Guide

CHAPTER 1: LIVING AN 80/20 LIFE

- In short, the Pareto principle or 80/20 rule states that eighty percent of all outcomes arise from just twenty percent of causes, i.e., in many phenomena there are "the vital few and the useful many." We can use this principle by focusing on the vital few and de-prioritizing the useful many.

- We can apply this principle to learning, improving skills, absorbing new information, and boosting memory. We need to avoid carelessly applying the rule to situations that don't warrant it, and learn to think strategically about how and why it works for each situation.

- You can apply the technique to selecting the most effective study methods and techniques (make a list of ten and choose only the two most effective ones), reading, learning languages, and memorizing new material. By identifying the most useful, relevant, or unifying principles behind anything you learn, you stay streamlined and organized.

- A related law/principle is the "eighty-five percent rule," which states that optimal learning occurs when individuals succeed or achieve the correct outcome around eighty-five percent of the time. Through an optimal mix of success and failure, we can differentiate between effective and ineffective approaches, allowing for learning and progress. Deliberately shape your learning process so that you have the optimal level of failure by varying the size, type, and difficulty of tasks, and the support you receive to complete them.

- You can apply the 80/20 rule to acquiring new skills. What you do is as important as what you choose not to do. Your goal is not to bypass effort, cheat, or avoid discomfort but to wisely budget limited resources.

- Master new skills by setting clear goals, identifying and mastering smaller sub-skills, pre-empting and preparing for unavoidable challenges along the way, and piecing the subskills together again as you go.

- To be efficient, constantly ask yourself: is what I'm doing bringing me closer to my goal? Pick one SMART goal, prioritize it, and be consistent in working toward that goal every single day. Hack away at the inessential.

CHAPTER 2: KEEP THINGS LEAN

- In lean, minimalist learning, we identify and focus on the twenty percent of a new task that is genuinely unfamiliar, and deliberately leverage the eighty percent we already have some pre-existing knowledge about.

- Leverage the way your brain already learns by meaningfully connecting new and unusual information to concepts you have already mastered. Start every new lesson with a mind map that captures what you already know, then scan the material to get a high-level overview of how it's organized. Finally, make deliberately vivid connections and associations between new and old, and revisit your original mind map to track progress.

- Being a minimalist learner is about thoughtful, value-driven, conscious consideration of new information, and a proactive attempt to structure your learning efforts to match. Minimalism often requires decluttering, but it's about the clarity and purpose behind what is removed and what remains, and not about *what* you're choosing to keep. Declutter your learning space, your mindset/attitude, and your routines, processes, and habits. Look at your life and remove what does not directly support your stated learning goals.

- Remember that your attention and awareness are your most valuable resources; you get to choose how you "spend" them. What is the least that needs to happen for you to make concrete progress toward your goal? Take concrete action.

- To minimize information overload, actively engage with new content and reflect on its relevance to your goals and values. Most data we encounter will be irrelevant to us, outdated, inaccurate, inappropriate, or flat out wrong. We need to continually identify what we need to know, how much we need to know, and its deeper value. Develop your informational boundaries. Finally, learn to recognize when information overwhelm is just low self-esteem or fear in disguise.

CHAPTER 3: LEARNING TO LEARN

- Your learning mindset matters because it determines your overall philosophy and approach and the techniques you use.

- Time is the most important resource, so be mindful of how you use it. The "five-hour rule" encourages us not to waste precious time on irrelevant activities, but spend at least an hour a day on meta-learning, reflection, and deep thinking. Commit to that hour and experiment with how you use it. Realize that the world is moving at such a pace that you need to learn continually just to stay relevant.

- Don't get distracted by the format of new material, but just focus on whether you're learning something new ("aha!") or you're stumped ("huh?"). Note down every "aha!" and "huh?" moment and work with them directly. Simultaneously get into the habit of creating a running one-sentence summary of all the new concepts you're learning. For difficult concepts, use the ADEPT method to increase understanding: For each concept find an analogy, diagram, example, plain English, and technical definition, in that order.

- Only twenty percent of study methods will yield eighty percent of your results, so use evidence-based approaches like active reading and notetaking, spaced repetition, distributed practice, interleaving, regular breaks, and mnemonic devices such as the "memory palace technique."

- When you are a self-directed learner, you create your own learning standards and your own learning philosophy, rather than looking to external standards to tell you what to value and why. Set your own goals and measure them by your own metrics. This makes you a more effective, sophisticated, and resilient learner.

CHAPTER 4: THE 80/20 RULE CAN SOLVE PROBLEMS

- The 80/20 principle can help us solve problems efficiently and find useful answers to the question: is what we're doing working? We can reframe any snags and obstacles in the learning journey as opportunities to check up on your strategy overall.
- The learning process continues even after you've reached your deadlines, written your exams, or met your goal. Evaluate the learning process itself so you can make useful adjustments and learn how to learn. By observing and reflecting on your

learning experiences, you can refine your study strategies and allocate your time and effort more efficiently.

- One way is to use the Kirkpatrick Model and analyze on four levels: initial reaction (how enjoyable you found it), learning (what you actually learned), transfer (how applicable the learning is more broadly), and results (what the outcome is compared against goals).

- When we hit a plateau and our learning stagnates, it's important to identify the twenty percent actions that will get us moving again—they're usually the scariest ones. Breaking through plateaus requires us to expose ourselves to new stimuli, take courageous action, and get moving again.

- To keep learning and developing, embrace discomfort and don't get complacent in gains you've already made and banked. Identify the Big Thing you're avoiding and tackle it head-on, switch up your technique and try something new, or push yourself to commit to a bigger and more ambitious goal.

- The Pareto principle can help us become efficient problem-solvers if we understand that eighty percent of our difficulty will come from just twenty percent of problems. Identify your problems, rank them by frequency, and solve the most frequent and impactful ones first. See problems as teachers; expect and welcome their lessons.

Made in the USA
Las Vegas, NV
15 November 2023

80891841R00095